"Accomplished author and journalist Marilyn Murray Willison, like so many of us, turned 65 and wondered what it all meant and where it all went: the dreams, the plans, the goals. In her new memoir she explores the twists and turns her fascinating life has taken, and comes to the conclusion that we over-65s need to let go of the old dreams and create new ones. *ONE WOMAN, FOUR DECADES, EIGHT WISHES* is an invaluable guide for all women. Especially for those who are ready to embark on the new exciting journey that awaits us."

Jane Heller, New York Times bestselling novelist and author of *YOU'D BETTER NOT DIE OR I'LL KILL YOU: A CAREGIVER'S SURVIVAL GUIDE TO KEEPING YOU IN GOOD HEALTH AND GOOD SPIRITS*

"Marilyn's poignant words speak to women of the Baby Boomer generation in an honest, compassionate and introspective way. If you are part of this growing demographic, you will surely be inspired and find validation in her words."

Nancy Davis, Founder of *Race to Erase MS*

"Any woman who has wrestled with growing older will celebrate what Marilyn Murray Willison has accomplished in her latest book. She has captured issues ranging from affection to employment to health and vanity with charm and honesty. I'll be enthusiastically giving *ONE WOMAN, FOUR DECADES, EIGHT WISHES* to all my girlfriends."

Connie Glaser, bestselling author and columnist

"In this engrossing memoir, the author's story made me realize that most of us take life and its riches for granted—until illness strikes or deteriorating health makes even ordinary things difficult. Marilyn's brave MS struggle shines through with clarity and intensity. I love her inspiring 'Never give up!' attitude."

Elisabeth Tretter, former Executive Editor, *MIRABELLA* magazine.

"Marilyn writes with lucidity and depth about finally crossing the Baby Boomer threshold of turning 65. Her memoir is interspersed with humor, struggles, triumph and wisdom. It's an honest, inspiring book that avid readers will both enjoy and use as a guide. Life's road is never straight, but somehow Marilyn navigates the course and invites us to take the journey with her."

Heidi Kingstone, author of *DISPATCHES FROM THE KABUL CAFÉ*

"I enjoyed reading *ONE WOMAN, FOUR DECADES, EIGHT WISHES* because every page held my interest. It is an inspiring memoir, and I know that countless other readers will benefit from—and be enriched by—sharing Marilyn's unique journey. The hours it takes to read this book is time very well spent."

Arnold Shapiro, Academy Award and Emmy Award winning producer of *Scared Straight, Rescue 911, Big Brother,* etc.

"Marilyn Murray Willison is an inspiration to many people. She is a powerful and kind spirit, and I loved reading *ONE WOMAN, FOUR DECADES, EIGHT WISHES.* "

Camille Grammer, former original cast mate of *The Real Housewives of Beverly Hills.*

One Woman, Four Decades, Eight Wishes

A Journalist's Memoir of Challenge, Change and Growth

Marilyn Murray Willison

For Marcia,
Thank you so much!

Marilyn

ISBN: 0982394101
ISBN 13: 9780982394106

ALSO BY

MARILYN MURRAY WILLISON

DIARY OF A DIVORCED MOTHER

TIME ENOUGH FOR LOVE

THE SELF-CONFIDENCE TRICK

WHEN YOUR LIFE INCLUDES A
WHEELCHAIR

THE SELF-EMPOWERED WOMAN

For

RAMON POZ

Con gratitude por los años de cuidado, amabilidad y sensitividad. Tu presencia alegre a hecho mejorar cada aspect de mi vida, y yo siempre estare agradecida.

(With gratitude for your years of care, enthusiasm, kindness and sensitivity. Your cheerful presence has made every aspect of my life better, and I will always be grateful.)

TABLE OF CONTENTS

Page

This I know:

> You can wake up to your higher self
> You can be patient and you can be kind
> You can be wise and almost whole
> You can walk out of hell and into the light
> You don't have to run away from life your whole life
> You can really live
> And you can change
> And you can be an agent of change

Laura Dern
(Amy Jellicoe)
HBO's *Enlightened*

INTRODUCTION

The real point of being alive is to evolve into the whole person you were intended to be.

Oprah Winfrey

When I first began working on this book, my intention was to examine (and then write about) how turning 65 had affected the millions of Baby Boomer women who—like me—found themselves caught off guard by the arrival of that milestone birthday. But as my research ballooned, what had begun as an analytical project gradually evolved into a mini-memoir about how practically everything in my own life had changed so drastically over the years.

Like many members of the Baby Boomer generation, I'd always thought of myself (apologies to Bob Dylan and Rod Stewart) as a person who would be *Forever Young*. And I definitely felt far too young to conduct—much less commit to paper—an emotional inventory of my life. But that fantasy slammed to a screeching halt when I came to the unsettling realization that in only a few short months I would be 65 years old. (Really? How could this be possible?). Not surprisingly, I experienced my own version of Elisabeth Kubler-Ross's five stages of grief: denial, anger, bargaining, depression, and (finally) acceptance.

Sixty-five has been our society's "traditional" retirement age, which meant it was synonymous with old age. Retirement used to represent what was considered the end of productivity and a dramatic dilution of worth. So, coming face-to-face with being a *bona fide* Senior Citizen opened the door to a year-long, reluctant reassessment of practically every aspect of my—evidently—"long, long" life.

I slowly—and reluctantly—began to realize that so many things that once had been of value in my life (i.e., the importance of being polite, dressing nicely, following "the rules," good grammar, newspapers, table manners, etc.), no longer seemed to have much relevance in today's world. Things that I'd once thought were rock-solid and non-negotiable had become not only outdated, but—yikes!—quaint. It was emotionally upsetting to come face to face with so many changes, and to realize (and be forced to accept) that neither my skills nor my values were in sync with those of today's world. Somehow, the "popular" or "dominant cultural" bandwagon had passed me by, and—at 65—I had somehow become an anomaly.

Obviously, embracing the fallout that accompanies reaching one's retirement age—as well as evaluating the accumulation of decades' worth of experiences—can be both confusing and difficult. And while working on this book, I learned that there were plenty of other people—all across the country—who were also wrestling with this uncomfortable and unwelcome (especially in light of The Great Recession) bout of both personal and professional reassessment. After all, between December 2007 and June 2009, 8.4 million jobs (over 6% of all payroll employment) were lost, which means that I have shared this soul-searching (and financially bruising) journey with millions of other Americans.

And even if our work/career shift hadn't been affected by the economy, the March of Time has managed to take its own toll on every other aspect of our lifestyles, as well. Only about 12% of Americans were of retirement age in 2013, but by 2030 the number of Senior Citizens will rise to more than 18%. In fact, researchers now predict that about 10,000 Baby Boomers will turn 65 every day until about 2029, and 50% of those are females. In other words, I am one of about 10 million American women who have—either because of age or economics—lost their once-comfortable "professional" place in the world.

In March of 2013, Erin Callan (the former CFO of Lehman Brothers) wrote an article for *The New York Times* about the challenges of rebuilding a life once one's career evaporates. She wrote, "I did not know how to value who I was versus what I did. What I did *was* who I was....Without the [financial] crisis, I may never have been strong enough to step away. Perhaps I needed what felt at the time like some of the worst experiences in my life to come to a place where I could be grateful for the life that I had. I had to learn to appreciate what was left."

During one of my recent self-evaluation sessions, I realized that my entire life had been full of countless non-stop (both major and minor) changes. So many elements of my younger, healthier life—jobs, goals, homes, significant others—are now dramatically different from what I had planned or expected. So many important things have shifted from *what was* to (now that I am 65) *what is*.

The one thing that had, however, not changed (whether I was taking a break from studying for an exam in California, having trouble falling asleep in Katmandu, or calming my nerves before boarding the Concorde en route to a major interview on another continent) was the mantra I had used for decades to diminish my anxiety and keep myself on track. Whenever I found myself on the verge of being overwhelmed by depression, fear, self-doubt or worry, I would silently drown out the negativity by mentally telling myself, *I am healthy, beautiful, loved, and enlightened; happy, famous, rich and thin.*

Little did I know that while the eight words that comprised my mantra would stay the same for decades, almost everything else in my life would be transformed. Through the years, the varied experiences that would come my way managed to quietly alter (and yet drastically change) each of my youthful "wish list" definitions.

As a freshman in college, I'd learned about the work of Emile Coué, a French psychotherapist, who managed to cure many of his patients (back in the 1920s) by using this motto: *"Every day, in every way, I am*

4

getting better and better." His patients were instructed to repeat these words 20 times, three times each day because Coué believed that constant repetition of positive thoughts could overpower (and eventually eliminate) negative ones.

As a budding young would-be perfectionist, I chose to be more specific about my wish list. So I replaced "better" with a wide-ranging variety of adjectives (*healthy, beautiful, loved, enlightened, happy, famous, rich and thin*) that seemed more relevant to my then-immediate concerns. Little did I know at the time that while the eight words that comprised my long-ago mantra would stay the same, the unexpected and unforeseen events of my life would drastically alter and transform both their definition as well as my "wish-list" perspective.

Back in 2006, Rhonda Byrne's book, *The Secret,* which publicized the concept of the law of attraction (i.e., focusing only on what you want) became an instant bestseller. Her book has sold more than 19 million copies, and she has joined a long list of "positivity" authors like, Napoleon Hill (*Think and Grow Rich*) and Norman Vincent Peale (*The Power of Positive Thinking*). Perhaps they were all acolytes of Buddha, who wrote, "*The law of the mind is relentless. What you think, you create; what you feel, you attract; what you believe becomes reality.*" And—as an optimistic acquisitive young woman—I was willing to bet that there was nothing to lose (and possibly much to be gained) by reminding myself—over and over and over again—of what I really wanted out of life.

5

This tailor-made mantra eventually morphed into my cast-in-stone, aspirational wish list. There was (and probably still is) a big part of me that truly, optimistically believed that if I repeated those eight adjectives (*healthy, beautiful, loved, and enlightened; happy, famous, rich and thin*)—preceded, of course, by "I am"—often enough they would surely become manifest in my life. The young me was convinced that I could somehow imprint these qualities on my subconscious by keeping them—year after year after year—in the forefront of my thought patterns. And that's how it grew to become my personalized (although wistful), long-running, Coué knock off.

Both my early retirement (for unpleasant medical reasons, but more about that later) and the arrival of that improbable 65th birthday taught me that just as my body had aged and altered with the passage of time, so had the very meaning and essence of the mantra that had been my customized emotional crutch for close to half a century.

I—presumably like countless others—had become increasingly change resistant with each passing decade. When I was young (much to my mother's chagrin) I embraced anything that was "cutting edge" or "new." In fact, for years I actually believed that the true definition of *improvement* was *change*. But gradually (like millions of old fogeys before me), I realized that I disliked the changes that came *to me* (like the unstoppable tsunami of technological advancement), but welcomed those that originated *within me* (like an updated and revamped value system). As the accoutrements of my younger self fell away—both personally and professionally—I eventually realized that not only had I changed, but that the time had come for me to actually consider being a reluctant, 65-year old, semi-subversive, agent of change for others as well.

As business writer Peggy Klaus once wrote about acknowledging her 60th birthday, "With aging, as with most things in life, attitude counts for a lot....You're only as old as you feel. So let's feel good about being [our age] and beyond. Let's even brag about it....We have much experience and wisdom under our belts, which makes for a distinct perspective and, ultimately, a richer culture. At this age, like any other, the key to happiness is to fully embrace who we are—to prize what we learn and to appreciate how far we've come."

Baby Boomers used to be referred to as part of a "pig-in-the-python" phenomenon, because there had never before been such a generational distortion. Although we are aging, there are more than 75 million of us, and despite the Great Recession, we still control 50 percent of discretionary buying power, as well as a whopping 80 percent of personal financial assets. And according to the experts, our generation is responsible for $2 trillion in consumer spending each year. So even if our employment levels and influential impact are waning, we have both changed and contributed to society in major ways over the past 50 years—and we still have unmeasured impact yet to come!

So why did I write this book? Because I feel that there are many women like me who have changed during (and been changed by) the passing years. Mine is just one small story of altered values and lessons about what it takes to adapt to a dramatically different way of life. But I also like to think of this book, which focuses on the unexpected impact of my 65th birthday, as one woman's modern-day survival story. Plus, as a journalist, after several decades of earning my living by writing about other people's life stories, I'm finally ready to take a much closer look at my own.

As Kelly Corrigan wrote at the beginning of *Glitter and Glue* (her moving memoir about change and growth): "This is a work of memory, and mine is as flawed and biased as any other. I was aided by dozens of…photographs, journals… and the Internet."

Once again, Oprah has found the perfect words to soothe the soul of a 65-year old. According to her, "Getting older is the best thing that ever happened to me. I wake up every morning rejoicing that I'm still here with an opportunity to begin again and be better." And, thanks to the combined efforts of the economy and Father Time, we are all lucky enough to be living in an altered—and ever-changing—21st Century World.

The good news is that—after revisiting the wildly diverse events of my life—I have something wonderful in common with millions of my Senior Citizen Sisters. Like them, I have earned the right to honestly celebrate the fact that the passage of time may have turned me into a truly transformed woman in more ways than I could have ever foreseen, but I am (almost miraculously) still me!

HEALTHY

CHAPTER 1

I am **HEALTHY**, beautiful, loved, and enlightened; happy, famous, rich, and thin.

Usually, we believe that our pain is a misfortune that needs to be fixed, but in fact, all pain (physical, mental, and emotional) is a necessary step towards becoming conscious.

Eliza Mada Dalian

There's no doubt about it—I was a lucky little girl. Perhaps it was genetics, or maybe it was some other factor, but I was always part of that enviable group of children who were consistently labeled by their pediatricians as being "robustly healthy." Other than a brief bout of whooping cough as a preschooler, the removal of my tonsils, and a three-day weekend bout with German Measles when I was 14, I honestly don't remember ever being ill as a youngster. From the first day of Kindergarten all the way through college graduation, I'm sure that I had fewer than a handful of "sick" absentee school days.

A therapist would probably say that this was an unconscious "avoidance reaction" to my parents' combined health challenges. As an adopted child, I was raised by an older couple who had (decades earlier) lost two toddlers to now-rare childhood diseases—diphtheria and scarlet fever. That trauma, combined with their own unfortunate health issues, was the reason why they were determined that I would simply never, ever be ill. There were many unspoken subliminal messages attached to my childhood, but the clearest (to my young mind, at least) was THOU SHALT NOT BE SICK!

They, on the other hand, never seemed to be free of some sort of physical challenge. Even today, I can clearly feel and remember the emotional discomfort I would experience whenever the normal rhythm of our home life was (all too often) disrupted by the illnesses of one parent or another. Health problems, to my young mind, seemed to always be the "no-fair" reason behind our family's cancelled activities, their emotional malaise, and the rescheduled play dates that almost always accompanied my parents' bouts of feeling "under the weather." My primary youthful job, therefore, was to consistently, reliably, be healthy and energetic.

Not surprisingly, for most of my childhood it was hard to not feel—both figuratively and literally—like I was being raised by grandparents from a different era. Unlike my friends' parents, Mama and Daddy didn't join clubs, ride bikes, go on ski trips or throw cocktail parties. On occasion, they would (much to my delight) waltz around the living room together if they heard one of their favorite songs on the radio, but their shared activity of choice was to sit in their easy chairs and smoke cigarettes while reading out loud to each other before bedtime.

My classmates had parents whose lives had been shaped by the events of World War II, but Mama and Daddy considered the Great Depression to have been the pivotal wrecking ball of their young adult years. They had been on their honeymoon when Black Friday—October 29, 1929—happened; he was 26 and she was 24. Stories about Hoovervilles, WPA, and the New Deal were part of the muted soundtrack of my youth. Their age, obviously, affected everything about them—not just their economic, historical, and political perspectives.

Mama's complaints about migraine headaches, muscle spasms and sinus infections simply became a subliminal type of chronic static during my teen years. And although I never—ever—heard him complain, Daddy's slow decline—from asthma to emphysema to lung cancer—meant that clusters of orange plastic prescription bottles played a major visual role in my childhood landscape.

*   *   *

I know only too well that for some people good health is all about athleticism, strength, vanity or even youthfulness. But for me it occupied an entirely different arena. Since my parents were plagued with what seemed like a laundry list of physical complaints, being overtly healthy practically became (for a chronic good girl who was too intimidated to smoke, drink, cut classes, or do drugs) my personal form of comparison-fueled teenage rebellion. While my peers may have experimented with controlled substances, curfew violations, or familial shouting matches, never getting sick was probably a perverse and private way for me to manifest a growing sense of independence from my parents' weary world of physical discomfort.

And although many of my Catholic girls high school classmates enthusiastically enjoyed wearing a candy striper's uniform while volunteering at the local hospital, I had no interest whatsoever in being anywhere near the same vicinity as illness. Naturally, many of those girls happily chose nursing as a career. But unlike my peers, I didn't want to work in a hospital—in part because while *their* adolescent heroes had been doctors and nurses and surgeons, *mine* had always been authors and editors and journalists.

My youthful focus on health, however, was actively alive and well—it just followed a different path from my friends'. Instead of feeling comfortable around the ill and wanting to learn how to relieve their distress, I wanted—even as a teenager—to better understand how to avoid being ill in the first place. And, as always, the easiest way for me to "research and resolve" this puzzling issue was to look for answers in books.

In college, when I probably should have been paying more attention to my upcoming French Literature mid-term exam on Stendahl's *Le Rouge et le Noir*, I was simultaneously turning the pages (OCD maven that I am, I would alternate the books I was reading chapter by chapter) of *The French Lieutenant's Woman* by John Fowles and *Let's Get Well* by Adelle Davis. Even when it came to magazines, I would be equally—irrationally— excited about the arrival of both *Prevention* and *Vogue*. To this day, I still haven't found more than one or two other friends (out of hundreds) who share my insatiable lifelong curiosity about what it takes to achieve and maintain good health.

As the years went by, my quest for (and the compulsive pursuit of) both a fulfilling career as a writer and a physically active—i.e., uninterrupted by illness— life progressed in tandem. As an avid reader since childhood, nothing seemed more glamorous to me than a career as the writer of words that would be read by others. What had started slowly (as editor of a sixth-grade newspaper), continued into high school and college newspapers. As a young adult, I was a stringer for publications like *Family Weekly* magazine (my first cover story!), *National Catholic Reporter*, and the *Christian Science Monitor*. I was finally asked (OMG) to start reviewing books on a regular basis for *The Los Angeles Times*, and—before I knew it—my byline had appeared on its Fashion, Travel, Op-Ed and View pages, as well.

A few years ago, Diane Sawyer gave a *"Master Class"* lecture on the OWN channel, and had this to say about having a career as a journalist: "The great thing about it is that there is no definition...Journalism is waking you up. It's reminding you that this is a big, vast exciting planet...It's loving a fact. Other than that it's your curiosity. It's what you bring to it...All the people I have met have influenced me...Every one [gave me] a different lesson."

Imagine how thrilling and miraculous it seemed when—a little over a decade after I'd graduated from UCLA—I was lucky enough to be appointed Health and Fitness Editor at *The Los Angeles Times* Syndicate. As with almost every other phase of my career as a journalist, I couldn't believe how fortunate I was to actually be paid (handsomely) to do something (i.e., learn about how the body works) that I would have happily done for free.

*   *   *

The downside to my burgeoning journalism career was that it was accompanied by plenty of personal booby traps, not to mention the fact that demanding jobs more often than not come with mega doses of stress. Plus, I had failed to remember the warning in Gail Sheehy's 1976 book *Passages,* which stayed on the bestseller lists for three straight years. According to her research, women under the age of 35 simply were not equipped to juggle a career, marriage and motherhood without serious consequences. And as much as I hated to simply be another single-mother statistic, my experience reflected Sheehy's findings to a T.

And that's how a woman who had spent her entire life envisioning herself as inherently immune to illness, learned that life is full of unanticipated and unwelcome big, ugly surprises. After two painful divorces, stress-filled single motherhood, the aforementioned pressure-cooker career, and a regrettable sorrow-fueled hiatus from taking care of my own health and wellbeing, life threw a major curve ball my way.

When my emotional and physical defenses were literally at their weakest, illness (in the most-unwelcome form of MS—multiple sclerosis) came knocking on my front door.

In America today, almost half a million people are living with MS. Multiple sclerosis is named after the "many scars" or lesions that affect brain tissue and/or the spinal column. These lesions can show up in a variety of places, which is why every case of MS is relatively unique. There are patients (like Montel Williams) who cope with severe muscle pain, some people (like Jack Osbourne) have fluctuating vision difficulties, others (like Meredith Vieira's husband, Richard Cohen) struggle with voice issues, and many (like Teri Garr and me) lose muscle strength and become wheelchair dependent.

I later learned that people who feel overwhelmed, helpless and depressed (as I did in early 1984) often suffer from a chronic exposure to cortisol, otherwise known as "the stress hormone." And as Lauren Kessler described it in her brilliant memoir *Counterclockwise*, "Overexposure to cortisol is like an express train to the nursing home."

The first sign that something was seriously wrong with my body came after a routine in-office procedure to remove bone spurs on my toes. The fact that I never walked normally again after that podiatrist appointment on Bastille Day 1984, is a clear message that my "uncomplicated" foot surgery was simply one stressor too many during that chaotic period of my life. Shortly afterwards, at the suggestion of a friend who'd been concerned by my unsteady gait and my toes' persistent numbness, I visited a neurologist. He performed a cursory examination, said that it looked to him as if I had MS, and then advised me to "go home and get all [my] affairs in order." I (quietly but understandably) freaked out. Not surprisingly, I left his Beverly Hills office in a state of shock, and as I maneuvered my way through the congested L.A. traffic, I cried all the way home.

Like most MS patients, I went through a lengthy period of what is known as the "relapsing-remitting" phase of this challenging disease. These are the blocks of time when you feel symptom free, and can tell yourself that you've (fortunately) dodged a really major bullet. This "limbo" phase is also one of the reasons why it often takes doctors so long to come to a definitive diagnosis. And it was during one of these "Thank God, I'm perfectly healthy again!" phases that I (bravely and optimistically) accepted an English major's dream job offer to relocate my little family to London, and work as a journalist on Fleet Street.

Ever since Sister Mary Josita had assigned Charlotte Bronte's *Jane Eyre* to our sophomore English class, I'd treasured the quote, "I remembered that the real world was wide, and that a very field of hopes and fears, of sensations and excitements, awaited those who had courage to go forth into its expanse...." This was, two decades later, the perfect chance for me to spread my wings, and experience a whole new level of achievement and challenge.

A potential extra bonus of this surprising career opportunity was that I would be able to give my sons the "priceless gift of an international experience." It was a scary move for the three of us on a variety of levels, but I will always be grateful that I had the opportunity to make it possible for them to visit Edinburgh, Madrid, Moscow, Paris and Switzerland, as well as have friends and classmates who'd come to London from a variety of countries all around the globe.

When Sir David English (who had the distinction of being a Fleet Street editor for an unprecedented twenty years) first asked me to consider moving to London, I was apprehensive about saying goodbye to so many aspects of my comfortable life in L.A. But over a long dinner at River Walk restaurant in Kingston Upon Thames— several months before my move—he regaled me with stories of his earlier years as a journalist in Moscow. He told me how it had enhanced his career beyond measure, and how his kids had grown—emotionally and intellectually—because of the experience.

Sensing my initial hesitation, he told me, "It's never easy to uproot yourself from the familiar, and I know it will be hard for you to leave *The Los Angeles Times*. Temporarily, it might be difficult for you to feel at home, and for your boys to get settled in their new school. But I promise you that living and working in a country that isn't your own is the equivalent of earning a Ph.D. in life. Trust me, and you will never regret the experience." In retrospect, I can honestly say that even in spite of the unknown challenges that lay ahead, Sir David's advice was spot on.

Sadly, the feared MS symptoms soon began to resurface. Only six weeks after we'd left L.A., I was walking on Kensington High Street with my two teenage sons when my legs let me know that I was really in trouble. Each step was a challenge, and emotionally I was torn between the panic I felt for myself, and the need to protect my sons from their mother's grim new reality. Several years after that first U.K. Saturday morning stumble, a battery of hospital tests, and an MRI confirmed that I had indeed just been enrolled in one of the planet's most emotionally and physically challenging classrooms.

Naturally, as the disease progressed, my mobility essentially ground to a halt. I was no longer physically able to effortlessly hop on a plane to Argentina, France, Ireland, or Italy. And those twice a year return trips to L.A. for movie-star interviews were simply no longer feasible; there was no way—with two uncooperative legs—that I could even think about driving safely. That's the compressed and short story of how my brilliant and much-cherished career as an international journalist painfully ground to a halt. The last cover story I wrote for a British magazine (while still living in London) revolved around my passage to New York from Southampton on the QEII. Even though it was spent in luxurious First Class comfort—the trip turned out to be five long days spent primarily by myself in my beautiful suite. By that time, the disease had made it simply too challenging and painful for me to walk around the (big) iconic cruise ship. It was the first—but definitely not the last—time that I was forced to develop heightened and refined mental skills as an obsessively thorough armchair researcher in order to compensate for my body's limited mobility.

*   *   *

Before I knew it, both my sons had returned stateside to continue their educations and I was alone—and very frightened—in a large Edwardian flat in Marylebone. By this point, just walking to the front door (or even from one room to another) had become a painful challenge. That's when I went through my own foolhardy form of seclusion and withdrawal. There were no more black-tie dinner parties or evenings in the West End because it was simply too challenging (and embarrassing) to try to get from point A to point B as others watched me struggle. I preferred to deny—or ignore—the fact that I was seriously ill, and chose to nurse my terror, sorrow, shame, and confusion in solitude.

But self-pity and sulking are coping mechanisms that—for an extrovert like me—could only last so long. Eventually, I came to the realization that living alone in isolation (while in a constant state of pain and panic) simply made no sense. So I accepted the situation, swallowed my pride, cried "Uncle," and returned to the U.S. I chose to settle in South Florida because of its surface similarities to the California of my youth, and then I worked diligently to build a miniaturized and disabled friendly version of my former comfort zone.

*   *   *

Even though (when I was a teenager) part of me had always rebelled against my parents' physical problems, there's no doubt that—when it comes to good health—I'm acutely aware of the fact that I actually owe a great debt to my stern long-suffering mother. She's the one who (by her iconoclastic example) introduced me to the potential benefits of alternative medicine. Evidently, at some point, she got tired of dealing with MDs who never seemed to help her feel better. Or, perhaps it was Mama's inbred respect for the ways of nature that was simply a part of her DNA from having grown up on a farm back in the early 1900s.

Whatever the reason, our home was the only one I was ever aware of (remember, this was back when JFK was president) that had numerous vitamin bottles, "starters" for homemade yogurt, and sour-dough bread fermenting on display in the kitchen, as well as a total absence of any pre-packaged, "instant" or fast foods. I now realize that my parents were way ahead of their time by—whenever possible—raising their own hormone-free chickens, tending small backyard gardens, and building large custom-made compost receptacles for our family's use.

So, as an adult, it's no wonder that I was more comfortable relying on my own fact-finding "health instincts" than blindly accepting whatever neurologists happened to tell me about living with MS. Back when Mama had tried to get healthier, female doctors (especially in the small towns where we used to live) were almost impossible to find. So years later—like her—I was too skeptical and independent minded to place all of my trust in the opinion of one white-coat wearing man.

And that's why (although it often surprises other people) in spite of the fact that I've had MS for three decades and been wheelchair dependent for 24 years, I've never taken any medication prescribed by a neurologist. Why? Primarily, because among the many lessons I learned from being Health and Fitness Editor during my Los Angeles newspaper days, I knew only too well about the inherently toxic nature of many prescription drugs—especially those used to address chronic conditions. So I immediately—almost as if on autopilot—rejected the prescribed steroids and other drugs suggested to me by a variety of well-meaning physicians.

Instead, I started road-testing alternative ways to try to proactively cope with MS. And when it came to nutritional programs, I reluctantly became familiar with alkaline, low-carb, Paleo, Swank, vegan, raw, as well as a variety of anti-inflammatory and cleansing diets. I also explored everything from acupuncture, CCSVI, chiropractic, colonics, Gyrotronic, massage, MELT, physical therapy, Pilates, STIM, Skenar, and even vitamin infusions. The result is that, after almost a quarter of a century in a wheelchair, MS still dominates my daily life even though (a) I'm told that I don't "look" like I have an illness, and (b) every single one of my other medical health markers are beyond impressive. Go figure!

Even though I'd originally been "diagnosed" with MS in Los Angeles back in 1984, after several years in London it was obvious that I was in need of additional medical input. So, in 1987, after my first MRI (which confirmed the brain lesions that are considered the gold-standard diagnostic confirmation for MS), my Harley Street neurologist gave me even more unwelcome news. He somberly informed me that the average life span for MS patients was 20 years from the date of diagnosis, which (he felt) meant that the year 2004 would be approximately the end of my inevitably difficult struggle. Obviously, I like to think that my healthy lifestyle and non-traditional drug-free approach to MS has made it possible for me to productively way outlive his doomsday prediction…

*   *   *

Back in the days when I worked as a journalist in London, I often felt like one of those long-ago performers on the *Ed Sullivan Show* who balanced numerous spinning dinner plates on thin wooden poles, and then frantically raced from one to the other to avoid creating a stage full of broken dishes. I was coping with the demands of a high-pressure job (which I really loved) in a—literally—foreign environment. I was a single mother coping with all the challenges that come with raising two teenage sons alone, and every member of my long-term and much-needed emotional support system was thousands of miles away on the other side of the Atlantic. In addition to all that, I was also battling a serious (and scary) chronic health issue.

One wintry day, I was absentmindedly walking from one end of *The Daily Mail's* editorial floor to the other, and winding my way past a sea of identical metal desks. Since I was one of the few women in that predominantly male environment, whenever I looked at the testosterone-heavy landscape of white shirts, receding hairlines, and cigarette smoke it was hard not to have a "We're not in Kansas anymore" moment. I was an obvious minority—by both gender and nationality—and it was obvious to everyone at the paper that my every move (and every story I filed) would be met with microscopic scrutiny.

That's why it was doubly cringe worthy when—on that damp chilly morning—I tripped (or perhaps I stumbled) and landed face-first flat on the floor in front of all my fellow editors and journalists. It only took me a moment or two to pretend that nothing important had happened, get back on my feet, dust off my then-fashionable "Dress for Success" women's navy blue business suit, plaster an embarrassed smile on my face, and (carefully) make my way back to the safety of my own metal desk. On the outside, I made it look as if I'd just had a silly, unfortunate, clumsy moment—but on the inside, I was deeply rattled. Embarrassment and fear of the future impact of MS were waging a nuclear assault on my psyche.

Two weeks after that stumble, I received another warning sign when I tried—again at work, again at that metal desk—to cross my right leg over my left. For the first time in my life, my body stubbornly refused to do what my brain had requested, and that became my physical introduction to the hated phrase "I can't."

*   *   *

Back in the days when I worked as a journalist in London, there were eleven competing newspapers, and time—as in deadlines—was always an issue. Those were the days (hard to imagine) before Blackberries, cell phones, computers, Smartphones, texting, etc. So when, for example, I would be assigned to interview, say,

Placido Domingo or John Malkovich, my editor—who lived in a highly anxious and fearful state of being "scooped" by another newspaper—would more often than not instruct me to "Just call in the story the minute he (or she) is out of the room." It was scary and intimidating to know that I had to quickly compose an article in my head—without the benefit of paper, pen or typewriter. But to keep up with the competition and hold my own, it was a skill that I simply had to master. And I did.

In those days, each London newspaper had its own noisy version of a room full of "copytakers." At *The Daily Mail*, that room was populated by a bank of crusty-sounding middle-aged men who sat at typewriters and transcribed dictated stories from reporters who called in from the field. I never actually had the chance to see or meet the people at the other end of the phone lines, but it didn't take long for me to recognize their voices or for them to recognize mine—after all, I was the only Yank on staff.

The longest article I ever filed by phone—which was dispatched from Argentina—was my 2,000-word, world-exclusive interview with Prince Andrew's future mother-in-law and her husband before his 1986 Royal Wedding. The transcription took place during a very long transatlantic phone call from my hotel room in Buenos Aires to the middle-of-the-night telephone bank back in London. In retrospect, it was a tedious process for everyone involved, but that's how things were done on Fleet Street back in the Margaret Thatcher era. Little did I know then that learning to compose a story in my head before dictating it to a typist would one day be the only way to keep my MS-ravaged career as a writer on life support. And it's the way that my Florida-based magazine and newspaper articles—as well as my last three books—were created.

As expected, my physical condition continued to slowly deteriorate, and by the time I was 42, I was completely wheelchair dependent. With great effort I could (barely) wiggle the toes on my left foot. And while I could move my right arm and make a fist, the fingers on that hand had permanently gone on strike, which meant that I was now a journalist who could neither travel nor type. My career, of course, was in shambles, my income had evaporated, and my medical expenses were growing like kudzu. And it was at just about this time when I came across Dorothy Parker's sardonic quote, "Money cannot buy health, but I'd settle for a diamond-studded wheelchair."

So, obviously, I got the message—loud and clear—that the days of taking my good health for granted were long over. And I have to admit that it was hard for me to not torment myself about the way that so many people (think self-indulgent Rock Stars or drug abusers) had unwittingly abused their bodies for years and years and years. On some strange hypothetical level, it just didn't seem fair that there was an entire population out there that had overindulged on alcohol, cigarettes, drugs and God knows what else, but was still able to use their limbs and continue enjoying life—while cholesterol-conscious, drug-free, smoke-free, former health and fitness fanatic me was left to cope with an uncooperative body and all the complications that go along with paralysis.

Instead of me telling my body what to do, from here on out—unless and until some sort of stem cell miracle appears—my body's neuromuscular network will be in control of how I live, and what I do. And that's why, during the last decade or so, I've put a lot of effort into "adapting" to my new normal. When I get the rare chance to write an article for *The Palm Beach Post* (my last was in connection with Annette Funicello's MS-related death in 2013), I celebrate. The long-ago days of having a twice-a-week newspaper column (like I used to have in L.A.) are over. I know it, and I'm well aware that mourning what I may have lost—or envying those who apparently haven't lost anything—is a dangerous and wasteful pastime.

*   *   *

When it comes to my current attitude towards health, the challenges I've faced have taught me how to work really hard to replace fear and frustration with vigilance. During one point, when I was feeling very fragile and depressed, Martin Seligman's book *Learned Optimism* changed my life. He believes that there are four factors that contribute to everyone's good health: eating well, exercising, not smoking, and optimism. That's why I get as much movement and physical therapy as possible, and—with the added bonus of intermittent fasting—I've managed to learn how to pay very close attention to (a) nutrition, (b) my body's exercise levels, and (c) the ever-fluctuating state of my emotional wellbeing.

And even though I have very little interest in doctor appointments for anything other than the bare essentials, when it comes to books there's no such thing (for me) as too much medical information. I have read—with unbridled enthusiasm—books written by a variety of forward-thinking physicians including Dr. Daniel Amen, to Dr. Joel Fuhrman, to Dr. Mark Hyman, to Dr. Alejandro Junger, to Dr. Frank Lipman, to Dr. Woodson Merrell, to Dr. Oz, to Dr. David Perlmutter, and practically any other open-minded, published health advocate. As if that weren't enough, I have a sprawling collection of what I label "Medical Memoirs," which includes first-person stories of people who have dealt with everything from Alzheimer's, to blindness, to cancer, to deafness, to disfigurement, to MS, to Parkinson's disease, and spinal cord injury.

A few months before he died, I was lucky enough to interview Christopher Reeve for *The Palm Beach Post*. He was in town to support the Hebrew University's Annual Leadership Educational Forum, and to raise money for their work on behalf of paralysis research. We had both (he because of a horseback riding accident and me because of MS) become wheelchair dependent at the age of 42. With his large electric wheelchair positioned next to my small one, we discussed the challenges that accompany losing control of one's body and—therefore—one's life. I showed up at his suite at the Palm Beach Four

Seasons Resort with a newspaper photographer and my husband, Tony. Reeve, who was connected to a ventilator, was surrounded by a number of aides who were part of his regular rotating health support staff of 18 people— nurses, physical therapists, etc.

Midway through the interview, when I asked him about the mental challenges of being paralyzed, he told me, "I've learned to ignore my moods, because I've learned that whatever mood I'm in at any given moment will change before too long. And I accept that for even being in a good mood....It's really just a question of putting it in perspective." Like most of us who are coping with a neurological nightmare, Reeve was openly frustrated by the barriers that have hampered stem-cell research, and he told me that while we need to remain optimistic, we also have to work hard when it comes to physical therapy in order to insure that our bodies will be ready when a cure for our disability finally does arrive.

Our entire afternoon together was simply beyond inspirational. From his level-headed approach to the problems we shared, to his determination to prove the "medical experts" wrong, he truly was a physical and emotional Superman. When my article about him was published, it closed with these words, "...Christopher Reeve is a bigger hero to me than ever. He managed to sweep me off my feet without moving a muscle."

Obviously, my definition of "healthy" today is light years away from what it used to be. And even though I may (officially) be labeled "profoundly disabled," in my mind—at least—I never see myself as someone who is ill. I may have had MS for thirty years, and I may need others to comb my hair, cut my food, get me dressed, or type the words that are in my head, but this retiree's intellect is still running on all twelve cylinders. And, fortunately, the rest of my (paralyzed) body is also managing to function far better than anyone could or would have ever predicted three decades ago.

Kris Carr's astonishing book and documentary *Crazy Sexy Cancer* gave me an entirely new way of looking at both the good and the unwelcome changes that MS has brought my way. The brackets (of course) are mine, but the insight—and the realization that living in a totally healthy body sometimes comes with emotional blinders—is all hers: "[MS]…is a teacher. I was asleep…before [MS] shook me awake."

I am still here, and I am still productive. I loved *Morning Joe's* Mika Brzezinski's book *Obsessed*, in which she reminded us that, "To be emotionally healthy you need to acknowledge what you bring to the table and feel good about it. It's a waste of time and energy to concern yourself with what other people have or can do."

And that's the kind of **HEALTHY** I want to be, now that I'm 65.

St. Bernardine's eighth grade championship basketball team,
kneeling on the far right

On the way to the stables, 1984

33

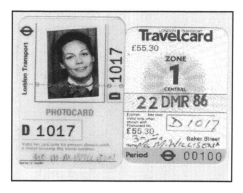

London Underground travel card and photo

My Daily Mail business card, 1985

At my Daily Mail desk, 1985

My Florida handicapped van license plate

With Christopher Reeve, 9 months before his death in 2004

BEAUTIFUL

CHAPTER 2

I am healthy, **BEAUTIFUL**, loved, and enlightened; happy, famous, rich, and thin.

A man's face is his autobiography. A woman's face is her work of fiction.

Oscar Wilde

I spent way too much of my youthful life wishing I were truly beautiful. As a young child, I knew that somewhere there was a world full of lucky little girls who were growing up surrounded by enchanted and admiring parents. These adults were—in my fantasy—continually reminding those fortunate little princesses just how pretty they really were. Alas, I was also both presciently and painfully aware of the fact that—for whatever reason—I would never be lucky enough to be part of that enviable approval-saturated universe.

This is the point of my story where I should tell you that neither of my parents had any interest whatsoever in aesthetics. Most of what had once been beautiful in their young lives had been brutally ripped away from them after the Stock Market crash of 1929, and after that financial trauma, their remaining energies had been diverted towards what was comfortable, practical and sensible. I honestly don't remember ever hearing my parents use adjectives like beautiful, elegant, luxurious, or sumptuous, because our homes' atmospheres were ones that fundamentally leaned towards the serviceable and the sparse. When I was growing up, far more attention was paid to the schedule for cleaning the ceilings than to the provenance of what little artwork decorated our walls. In other words, it almost seemed as if—to them—beauty represented a best-forgotten (and now a painful) luxury that they were no longer able to afford or enjoy.

Additionally, my no-nonsense mother truly believed that there were about a million other things that were far more important for her to worry about than whether or not her daughter's personal appearance was praiseworthy or stylish. After all, the basis of her value system was twofold: (a) The belief that children (i.e., me) should be grateful, obedient, and well-mannered—in other words "seen but not heard," and (b) the conviction that cleanliness really was next to godliness. I may have hungered to have been told that I was pretty, but whenever I was brave enough to ask, her terse reply would invariably be "Pretty is as pretty does." Therefore, her opinion of my behavior would always and forever trump what—in our family's vernacular, at least—was merely considered to be an inconsequential accident of genetics.

When it came to Daddy, even though it was no secret (from me or anyone else) that he thought I was within spitting distance of perfection, in his book my looks were essentially unimportant. So, with parents like that, it's no wonder that the attention so many other little girls effortlessly received for being cute or pretty, simply didn't exist during my childhood. Appearance-based compliments were foreign words to my young ears. And, unfortunately, my childhood's soundtrack actually grew into a slow but steady maternal drumbeat about what Mama honestly believed was "wrong" with the way I looked.

I was born in Portland, Oregon in late 1948, but my State-issued birth certificate is dated 1953. As I mentioned in the previous chapter, I was adopted as a pre-schooler by an older childless couple. Whether the apocryphal story that I later heard was true or not may never be known, but I was—as an adult—told that when I was an infant my "Portlandia" birth mother (who already had children) asked a close girlfriend to take care of me for a day or two. The woman who gave birth to me and her husband (who was—yikes!—evidently not my father) were having domestic troubles and, as the hard-to-believe story went, she and her family simply disappeared, and never came back to "retrieve" me.

Supposedly, my birth mother's girlfriend, who ran a bed and breakfast, didn't have the heart to take me to an orphanage right away because she always believed that one day her friend would come back for me. Meanwhile, Mama and Daddy were living down in Southern

California, missing their deceased much-loved toddlers, and wishing that they could somehow once again be parents. Since Mama had endured an emergency hysterectomy, and adoption agencies considered them "too old to qualify," they had essentially given up on their dream of parenthood.

Then, to continue the fairytale-like story that Mama told me after Daddy died, everything suddenly changed. The property title insurance company where Daddy worked asked him to go to Portland, Oregon to open a small out-of-state office. During that time he just so happened to lodge at the affordable bed and breakfast where I was living with my birth mother's long-suffering, loyal and patient girlfriend. Much to my everlasting good fortune, he fell head over heels in love with the little toddler (that would be me) who serendipitously happened to call that B and B her home.

Everything changed when, at some point, the nice owner of the bed and breakfast told Daddy that, unfortunately, she was going to have to send me to an orphanage before too long because I was becoming far more of a responsibility than she could handle on her own. And that's when he came up with the hypothetically perfect solution for all of us. After what must have been some serious discussions between the two of them, he— as the story went—immediately travelled to the Western Union office and sent Mama a telegram that essentially said, "GET ON THE NEXT TRAIN TO PORTLAND STOP, I HAVE FOUND US A DAUGHTER."

And so I went, as a precocious preschooler, to live with the couple who—for close to two decades—made me the center of their pre-retirement, well-meaning universe. Regardless of the scars (or stars) that I acquired during my continuously supervised march towards maturity, they remain—for totally different reasons—the true (but oppositional) heroes of my life story.

So, however bizarre this apocryphal story may sound today, the bottom line is that life changed dramatically in the 1950s for my quiet, small, stern, and once red-haired (hot tempered) new mother. She'd had my extroverted Humphrey Bogart-ish father all to herself for a long, long time and then I—the junior partner of an openly-smitten mutual admiration society—appeared on the scene. Naturally, we all learned rather quickly that when it came to our new cobbled-together little family, three was a crowd.

It's only fair to admit here that during the early days of my parents' marriage they had shared two passions—ballroom dancing and going to the movies. Or, as they called them, "picture shows." During those years, Mama (especially) became cinematically attached to the (now deceased) child actress, Shirley Temple, who—between the ages of three and twelve—had starred in an amazing 44 movies. There is no doubt in my mind that when Mama boarded the train that took her from Pasadena to Portland, in her imagination, a pint-sized, blond, blue-eyed little charmer would be waiting on the platform to smother her with hugs and kisses at the end of her long trip.

Of course, I'd already had several weeks to "bond" with the kind man who was determined to become my father. All the pretty new clothes and shoes that magically appeared when his wife arrived on the scene were amazing. But her simultaneous (and deeply disappointed) declaration that my hair was "all wrong" took precedence over the beautiful fur-trimmed pastel-blue wool coat that I never wanted to take off. And, for the next 20 years—via both subtle and overt means—Mama managed to find countless ways to continually remind me that I was (sigh) no Shirley Temple.

What soon followed our initial introduction was an uncomfortable wrestling match with a smelly, stinging home permanent that was supposed to shape my thick black hair into a mass of shiny long curls. I was too dark (and too wary) to be a smiling Shirley Temple clone. But as a Kentucky-born, Southern Belle manqueé, Mama was (almost) willing—if she could just get my long straight black hair to cooperate—to settle for a potential Bonnie Butler *Gone With The Wind* knock off.

*   *   *

In retrospect, I can now see that it was actually beneficial to have had her life-long critical nature focused in my direction, because it balanced out Daddy's always-adoring gaze. I shudder to think of what a conceited

42

egomaniacal mean girl I might have become without the yin and yang that their opposing perspectives provided. Still, girls really want (and even need) their mothers' approval, but hers was simply buried too deeply for me to ever feel either cherished or pretty.

As the years went by, I was taught (by her) that my complexion was too dark, my forehead too high, my hair both too black and too thick. Plus, my fingers, hands, feet, and legs were—unfortunately—simply too big for me to ever qualify as "beautiful." Oh, and on top of all that, I was—in her opinion—annoyingly clumsy, too much of a tomboy, and both my singing and speaking voices were irritatingly way too loud as well.

Although her words did—of course—hurt, I had fortunately been blessed with some sort of invisible Teflon shield that allowed me to categorize her maternal criticisms as opinions rather than facts. Plus, I wasn't emotionally destroyed by her fault finding because "being beautiful" had been a distant and diluted imaginary dream, rather than a top-of-the-list youthful priority. Thanks to Daddy, I had been raised to believe that what I did would *always* be more important than how I looked. He continually reminded me that while I might not have had any control over my complexion, the color of my eyes, the texture of my hair, or my height, I did have control over my achievements, my behavior, and my values.

The only "beauty" advice that Mama ever gave me was pretty succinct. She—who had not been beautiful even when younger—still felt strongly that it was important for every woman to pay very close attention to her complexion. As a result of that emergency hysterectomy when in her late 30s, she'd lost a great deal of weight immediately after her surgery. The result—back in the days before Botox, cosmetic fillers and laser treatments—was that she had far more facial wrinkles than most women of her age. So her oft-repeated message to me was that if I didn't want my face to look like hers (which I didn't), it would behoove me to avoid cigarettes, never get sunburned, sleep on my back, and never—ever—skimp on quality skin care.

Of course, as an inveterate researcher, I eventually began to look for other input, and started to conduct my own amateurish teenaged study of what beauty was, why it was so important, and how an insecure, ordinary-looking girl like me could capture it for herself. Eventually, that curiosity led to a relatively serious study of what beautiful women did to get—and stay—that way. A small mountain of books and magazines soon gave me a wealth of advice, pointers, and tips—many of which I absorbed, but most of which I managed to ignore.

The bottom line was that, as a young girl, beauty—of any sort—was not something that I had been able to learn about at home. But I was lucky enough to stumble across (or attract) a wealth of generous friends, mentors, and teachers who were enthusiastically willing to help me learn my way around the essential hallmarks of antiques, art, dance, fabrics, fashion, food, languages, and music. And thanks to their kind and thorough tutelage, I—

blessedly—stopped listening for parental compliments and looking for beauty in my mirror. Instead, I began learning how to find it in my surroundings, and wherever I happened to look.

*   *   *

Can you imagine—after that sort of ego-bruising childhood—how surprised I was when (as a teenager), I occasionally began to receive unexpected compliments on my appearance? For years, the American public (much like Mama) had considered "The Breck Girl" shampoo advertisements in magazines to be the perfect feminine ideal. But suddenly, in a Southern California world that had long-worshipped the blonde surfer-girl standard, my high cheekbones, olive-toned skin and long dark hair gave me some sort of "pseudo-exotic" free pass during the (first) era of Cher. I did—and always would—have far more in common with Ali MacGraw than with Christie Brinkley, and I milked whatever unexpected admiration I received for all it was worth. Finally (finally), I'd reached the point where there seemed to be plenty of nice people in my world who didn't want to change a single thing about the way I looked.

It was a gloriously enjoyable state of affairs for a young woman who had—for so, so long—felt inherently (visually) wanting. A *New York Times* essay by Andrew O'Hagan captured that treasured time in my life—this is what he had to say about the subject of beauty: "There's

45

something fantastic about the beauty of youth—the spectacle of a new person suddenly arriving at their physical peak. And we can celebrate that happy accident for what it is: a case of time and nature working pleasingly to an individual's advantage. But beauty in youth requires nothing of the possessor. It is only later that we expect the woman to step in, to take over, to augment that initial, guileless attractiveness with something deeper: confidence, instinct, self-knowledge, style, upon which lasting beauty depends."

Most women say that they looked their prettiest on their wedding day. But the closest I came to feeling "beautiful" was on February 28th, 1983, the night when my second husband and I had dinner with Queen Elizabeth and Prince Philip on board the Royal Yacht *Britannia*. There were 54 other guests—from Betsy Bloomingdale, M/M Francis Ford Coppola, M/M Bob Hope, M/M Carl Sagan, M/M Frank Sinatra, etc., etc., etc. At 34 years old, I was the youngest guest, and attending the royal banquet—complete with curtsying to the Queen and a dinner served by formally dressed footmen—was the ultimate Cinderella/Downton Abbey experience of my life.

I thoroughly enjoyed my happy state of deferred youthful vanity all the way through my 20s and 30s. And while I might have never been the prettiest woman in a room, still—possibly because of my attention to and obsession with beautifully made flattering clothes—I was fortunate enough to never go hungry for either male attention or female approval.

So, from my junior year of high school up until the time in my 40s (which was when my limbs stopped working), I managed to be relatively satisfied with the way I looked. And then my reliance on a wheelchair abruptly erased all the vanity and self-confidence that I'd worked so hard to acquire. Back in 1993, I wrote an article for *Allure* magazine about how the loss of my mobility had seemed to instantaneously overpower my former (hard-won and much-missed) attractiveness: "Once I came to terms with my limited mobility, I was struck not so much by how the wheelchair changed my view of life, but by how much the wheelchair affected the way I was viewed by others…how incredibly wasteful and sad it is that a few pounds of metal and vinyl can so quickly erase a person's attractiveness or invalidate his or her potential appeal."

Occasionally, back when I was writing for *The Los Angeles Times*, I'd had the chance to work on a beauty-oriented article—perhaps about a revolutionary skin care regimen, Henson Kickernick underwear, or a popular new Beverly Hills hair stylist. And only a few years ago, in Florida, I was able to compile a six-part "Makeover Marilyn" newspaper series in which I was the guinea-pig journalist for a variety of services that included hair highlights, laser skin treatments, teeth whitening, exfoliating facials, and so on. It was fun while it lasted, but—in my (very) age-dependent opinion—the whole experience of continual fussing and primping became tedious far before it probably should have.

While I was being "groomed and improved" for the *Palm Beach Post* series, I learned that no fewer than five of my girlfriends had treated themselves to plastic surgery procedures—ranging from a brow lift to a chin implant to several full face lifts! Wow. Since I had neither the money nor the machisma to get within close proximity to a plastic surgeon's scalpel, I knew that I would have to make peace with the "me" that I saw in the mirror. After all, hadn't Abraham Lincoln said something along the lines of "By the time you're 40, you have the face you deserve"?

During my long-gone days as a journalist, I'd had a king's ransom worth of opportunities to meet (both personally and professionally) beautiful women. In fact, a few of them were so naturally attractive—actresses Stephanie Beacham, Jennifer Connelly, and Jill Ireland immediately come to mind—that I would find myself practically staring at their beautiful skin, perfect features and warm smile. On more than one occasion I had to silently remind myself to quit gawking and get back to the business at hand.

*　　　　*　　　　*

This would be the ideal time to share one of my all-time favorite "walk down memory lane" experiences as a journalist. As I've probably mentioned before, back in the late-1980s, I was working in London, and my articles appeared in a variety of different British magazines and newspapers. I can't remember how we were introduced, but I do remember taking a long walk on a windy afternoon with the now-legendary Glenda Bailey. These days, she's famous for being (since 2001) the wildly successful Editor-in-Chief of *Harper's Bazaar* magazine. But back then she was known in the UK for her work on two popular and very hip publications, *Honey* and *FOLIO*. We met that day because she had just been chosen to be the Editor of the first English-language edition of *Marie Claire* magazine, and she was looking for a reliable and experienced journalist who could land a big name interview for the first-issue "launch" of her new magazine.

Fortunately, I'd been "in the business" long enough to have made a number of pretty powerful contacts, and I decided that this was the perfect time to call in a few favors. Three phone calls later, I'd been assured that I could have an exclusive interview with Audrey Hepburn—as long as I could guarantee that she would be able to talk about her work as a United Nations UNICEF Ambassador. Glenda was delighted with the news, and the arrangements were made for me to arrive—without a photographer—at the movie star's suite at the Savoy Hotel the following month.

we've been given. And it doesn't hurt to be grateful for whatever that big or small blessing might happen to be.

It's no secret that I have happily read countless books either by or about women who have led unconventional lives—the topic is one of my many obsessions. And even though I was only in my twenties when I first stumbled across *Madame: An Intimate Biography* (about the life of Helena Rubenstein), I never forgot her acerbic quip, "There are no ugly women, only lazy ones."

The talented journalist Peggy Orenstein, who wrote *Cinderella Ate My Daughter*, brilliantly captured my recent—if complicated—sentiments about beauty when she wrote "...what I find beautiful in other women is their charisma, their passion, their life force, not their poreless skin or slender midsection (well, OK, I still envy the slender midsection). It just might be time to apply those standards to myself, to disrupt my endless cataloging of faults, to stop dwelling on what I'm not—on what I will never be—and, finally, to revel in the genuine beauty of who I am."

Now that I'm officially a Senior Citizen, I'm also finally able—thank heavens—to accept that it's simply not my place to be the judge of whether or not I am (or I look) beautiful. Fortunately, however, I have learned the lesson that haunts all self-conscious women, which is— instead of focusing on what one sees in a mirror—to finally be able to (once and for all) actually feel **BEAUTIFUL**.

And what—for a currently unemployed, formerly insecure, temporarily vain 65 year old female—could possibly be better than that?

My first grade photo

Los Angeles Times headshot photo,
1985

On my way to dinner with Queen
Elizabeth and Prince Philip, 1983

Book Jacket photo for
The Self-Confidence Trick, 1988

Styled for my Allure Magazine
photo shoot, 1993

LOVED

CHAPTER 3

I am healthy, beautiful, **LOVED,** and enlightened; happy, famous, rich, and thin.

I am grateful to have been loved and to be loved now and to be able to love...because love liberates

Maya Angelou

I am acutely aware of the fact that—when it comes to being loved—I have very little to complain about. In fact, at times it almost feels as if I've been the recipient of far more than my fair share of affection.

While it's true that the first few years of my life were (unfortunately) a bit emotionally complicated, I know only too well that my situation could have been much, much worse. Still, I do regret that my parents did not have a *Little House on the Prairie*-type of happy spousal relationship. And—possibly because of our tension-filled home—which was not an oasis of calm affection, it has always been a challenge for me to fully grasp the concept of calm unconditional love. Even today, I still carry the ragged remnants of the mistaken belief that "love" is sort of like a sought-after prize or a reward that can—with the right amount of effort—somehow be earned.

The good news, however, is that (I truly believe) those of us who were born into chaotic situations, often receive an internal compensatory coping mechanism. It doesn't eliminate the blows to the ego or the heart, but it definitely dilutes and softens their impact. It's a little like what Tina Turner was talking about when Oprah interviewed the star after her wedding (at 73!): "I didn't know what love was as a young child, but I was born independent."

And, God knows, I have always had a pretty vibrant independent streak as well. My emotional independence seemed to be rooted deep within my DNA. As a youngster, I grew up without grandparents, aunts, uncles or siblings. Daddy died when I was only 19, Mama when I was 25, and by the age of 30, I was a confused and frightened divorcee with two small sons. The upside of that sort of instability is that autonomy is a priceless thing to have for keeping you on course and helping you to survive the tough times. But—as a number of my friends and I have learned the hard way—that type of emotional independence can also be an expensive liability when it comes to romance.

*　　　*　　　*

　　Back when I was a much-younger woman, and was preoccupied with my wish-list yearning to be "loved," what I think I really wanted—especially after two (!) painful divorces—was to have a romantic partner who would actively cherish me. I'd endured several hurtful and yearning years (during which I was actually part of a so-called "couple") when I was genuinely—almost physically—hungry for signs of a loved one's approval and appreciation. Unfortunately, all of that happened several decades before Joel Osteen advised his readers that, "You cannot waste your time trying to get something from someone that they're never going to give you." So I kept chasing after—and searching for—that ever-elusive true commitment.

　　Ok, here's a confession about how much I hungered to be the center of someone's universe. Do you remember the Linda Ronstadt and James Ingram 1987 hit song "Somewhere Out There" from the Steven Spielberg movie *American Tale*? Well, I was on one of my "Interview A Celebrity" business trips to L.A., had just finished a beautiful dinner in Beverly Hills, and was returning to my hotel late at night. I had just driven the rental car into the parking structure, and as I pulled into my space that wistful love song came on the radio. The realization that not one single person—out of billions—on the entire planet cared about or felt that way about me brought stinging tears to my eyes. And (in full singleton sorrowful mode) that's when—alone and surrounded by

61

hundreds of empty cars and a coal-black sky—I placed my forehead on the steering wheel, and in a flurry of self-pity, cried (and then cried some more) for what seemed like hours.

In the past, I had (fortunately) been wooed and won by a number of both remarkable and impressive men, each of whom had been—however temporarily—attractive, charming, generous and successful. But—to a man—they had all (some sooner, some later) made it clear that they were not going to be my Mr. Right. Sadly, it was way too easy, whenever I would sink into the depths of despair over one or another of those painful breakups, to tell myself that (like Othello) I had again loved "not wisely but too well." After all—years before—I'd identified with these words from Jane Austen's *Persuasion* much too closely, "But the one claim I shall make for my own sex is that we love longest when all hope is gone."

I had trusted—and offered my heart to—men who simply couldn't give me what I needed. It hurts to be "left behind," but the optimist in me kept looking (and looking) for love. As the well-respected Dallas preacher Bishop T. D. Jakes once observed, "When someone betrays you, your emotions are homeless." And for way too long I felt (and lived with) that free-floating torment in—literally—the worst way.

*   *   *

To honestly write about my "romantic history," I need to pause and include a brief tribute to a particularly lovely and amazing man from my past—Sir Gordon Reece. Gordon and I met in L.A. shortly before my second marriage imploded, and our paths often crossed again during the city's celebration-filled months that led up to the 1984 Olympics. I was busy with my hospitality assignments for the British Equestrian team, Gordon was busy spearheading Armand Hammer's public relations needs (which included major Olympic Games involvement), and we soon began to see each other socially more and more frequently.

What began as a casual semi-professional friendship soon blossomed into an enviable and exciting romance. Although he wasn't tall, Gordon was definitely a larger than life persona. For years, he had promoted and shaped Margaret Thatcher's image—from her hairstyle to the tone of her voice and even her wardrobe—and, as a result, had become one of her most trusted advisors and confidants. He spent every Christmas with the Thatchers at the Prime Minister's country home, Chequers. You may remember a scene in the Meryl Streep movie "The Iron Lady" in which she is being coached and drilled on her diction before delivering a major speech. Gordon—who was slim, fastidious, and paid close attention to his handmade John Lobb shoes and his Savile Row wardrobe—would have been appalled to see Roger Allam's portrayal of him as an overweight advisor who wore an ill-fitting dark blue suit and a nondescript necktie.

So, being a part of Gordon's world involved lavish and unexpected treats like weekends at stately West Green House (Lord McAlpine's country home), Sunday afternoons spent on horseback, champagne in his box at The Royal Opera House, and dinners at The Connaught. Gordon was brilliant, charming, generous and romantic, but he was also much too aware of his own magnetic appeal to ever be satisfied with the love of just one (hopelessly devoted) woman.

During our time together, Gordon was unfailingly elegant, kind and thoughtful. And in spite of his "romantic wanderlust," when it came to our relationship, this remarkable suitor was a true (even chivalrous) gentleman. When he flew from London to visit me—the former sweetheart with whom he'd spent hours on horseback at a variety of different stables—he was emotionally unprepared for what he saw. Once Gordon realized that I was totally incapable of moving out of my wheelchair, his formerly roving eyes were undeniably full of tears.

It was a lengthy, wonderful love affair that slowly ended with a sad whimper, but evolved into a mutually cherished "special friendship" that lasted until his untimely death from an inoperable brain tumor in 2001. At his funeral, the eulogy was delivered by Margaret Thatcher.

*   *   *

On one of my London newspaper assignments, I was asked to travel to Tim Rice's country home and interview the brilliant wordsmith who had given us a variety of memorable musicals, ranging from *Joseph and the Amazing Technicolor Dreamcoat,* to *Jesus Christ Superstar* and *Evita.* Naturally, I was in awe of him, and returned to London with my head full of music. Perhaps that's why, later, when I really wanted to torture myself about "the men who went away," I'd rely on the "*I Know Him So Well*" lyrics from Rice's 1984 West End Musical *Chess.* Even though the interview was one of my favorites, I still don't have a clue about how he was able to put himself—so brilliantly—in the minds of rejected, heartbroken women:

> *Nothing is so good it lasts eternally*
> *Perfect situations must go wrong*
> *But this has never yet prevented me*
> *Wanting far too much for far too long*
> *Looking back I could have played it differently*
> *Won a few more moments who can tell...*
> *No one in your life is with you constantly*
> *No one is completely on your side*
> *And though I moved my world to be with him*
> *Still the gap between us is too wide*

*   *   *

Fortunately (or maybe I mean miraculously), in spite of all the heartache and romantic disappointment, I never became a gender-blaming angry man-hating "dumpee." Instead, I managed to convince myself that lasting love—or having a healthy romantic relationship—required attitudes and personality traits that (here comes the adoption issues again) I simply didn't have. As I put it in a newspaper article that I wrote about love back in 2005, "...I'd essentially convinced myself that people with a happy marriage simply had access to a different, enviable 'skill set' that was somehow out of my grasp."

Accepting the blame may have been just one more way of unwittingly punishing myself, but it's also probably why all my former sweethearts (with only one exception) has remained a kind, positive, supportive friend. Even my second ex-husband—who had left me to move in with another woman—let everyone know that leaving me was, without doubt, the biggest mistake of his life. He so regretted our breakup that over the years before his unexpected death from a heart attack he crossed the Atlantic five times (!) in hopes that we would reconcile. I didn't want to sign up for a second round of instability, but I couldn't help but appreciate his misplaced (if ill-timed) ardor.

Dr. Gary Chapman's phenomenal book, *The 5 Love Languages,* had not been published back in the days when I was desperately trying to understand how to hold onto love. After working as a marriage counselor for years, and weary of listening to couples complain about "no longer feeling loved," Chapman researched the most common causes that led to breakups. His findings revealed that there are five different ways that humans express their affection and regard for each other: (1) Words of Affirmation, (2) Quality Time, (3) Receiving Gifts, (4) Acts of Service, and (5) Physical Touch. His book was published in 1995, has been translated into 38 languages, and for close to 20 years has progressively sold more copies than the year before. Obviously, it would have really helped me (and those unfulfilled relationships) to have understood the "science" behind lasting love.

*   *   *

Here is where I should write about a different type of affection—the love I have for my two sons. They were unwilling witnesses to their mother's strange and complicated love life, and for that I owe them a huge apology. When they were little boys and thought that they had the best Mom in the world, I assumed that they would always feel that way, and we would have unlimited amounts of time to be together. I can remember spending happy hours standing at the stove in our suburban-L.A. kitchen while baking cookies or making fudge. (This was long before I'd learned about the dangers of high-glycemic carbs!) I would stir what I was making, and fantasize about how our family would celebrate—and how I would cook their favorite dishes—whenever the boys (in the years to come) would return home from college.

Little did I know back then that by the time they would be old enough to go to college, I would no longer have that house for them to come home to—and standing anywhere (much less in front of a stove) was something I would simply no longer be able to do. One of the truly hurtful collateral-damage effects of a chronic illness like MS is that the relationships you value most are the ones that are sure to be irreparably altered—and rarely in a good way.

So now I am one of millions of aging, long-distance mothers who have children with homes that are far, far away from where we live. Like so many others, I am now one of those Florida grandmothers who—for a variety of reasons—must understandingly accept the fact that I am lucky to be able to see my sons (plus their beautiful families) for a once-a-year weekend visit. Of all the items I miss—on that lengthy list of once-cherished things that MS has maliciously taken from me—the one that hurts the most is the long-ago enviably close connection I used to have with those two little boys. The ones I celebrated and considered so very special, who are now accomplished, amazing, grown men with children of their own. But I—more than most—know only too well how confusing, painful and uncomfortable it can be to have a parent whose health is compromised and whose life is complicated.

I consider it part of my great good fortune that my sons (and their remarkable wives) have blessed me with four spectacularly perfect grandchildren. And even though—for some unknowable reason—fate has seen to it that we rarely get to be together, I optimistically dream of a future time when my health will somehow allow me to become a vital thread in the fabric of their lives. When I do get to spend time with my grandson and my three granddaughters, I am (probably like every other grandmother on the planet) overwhelmed with wonder and delight. So—when it comes to the hours that we do manage to share—I have chosen to cherish the quality, and forget about the quantity.

*　　　　*　　　　*

As part of the research for this book, I recently unearthed my old early-adult scrapbook, and was amazed at the handwritten love letters and protestations of affection that were hidden inside. Declarations of "everlasting love" had been glued to its now-disintegrating pages, and promises of a never-ending future together reminded me of my long-ago youthful, trusting belief in love. A few short decades later, a self-protective and somewhat-jaded me would often tell confidants that I was no longer interested in being "loved" because it almost always turned out to be either dangerously disappointing or merely fickle. Instead, I used to tell my friends, it was safer to spend one's energy working at being "admired"—the risk was smaller, and the payoff seemed greater.

In a 2013 essay about her own struggles with learning about illness and affection, Joyce Wadler, the author of *Cured: My Ovarian Cancer Story*, wrote about true love. "Love does not come as expected in a cancer hospital. I had seen this a few years earlier, sharing a room with a woman who was dying. She looked like what I had once thought cancer looked liked: emaciated, skin and bones. Her husband was with her. In the middle of the night the woman moved her bowels. The sharp stink of it pervaded the room. Her husband stayed by her side and murmured comforting things and emptied the bedpan, and I…thought that this is what real love is and how different it is from what you think love is when you are 22 and what you see in the magazines: the romantic dates; the sexy lingerie; the beautiful young woman; the rich, handsome man helping her out of the expensive car. Love was emptying the bedpan. Love was sleeping in a chair."

*　　　　*　　　　*

Now here's where my story about being loved takes a really sharp turn. After experiencing several unsatisfactory romances (not to mention the arrival of a seriously grim health situation), it was time for me to make some big changes in my life. So I reluctantly left London, and moved my beloved books, my treasured antiques, as well as that essential (but despised and unwanted) black vinyl wheelchair into a small Florida bungalow. The days of two-story Colonial homes, backyards brimming with fruit trees, or spacious Edwardian flats with marble bathrooms were long gone.

70

Anyway, in January 1997, a potential client for my at home book-editing services rang my doorbell, and then managed to change my life forever. Not surprisingly, the possible book project that brought us together never did get finished, but within six months of his first homework assignment, Tony—now my husband—had managed to quietly and persistently make himself an indispensable part of my new, restructured life.

You should know that Tony wasn't the type of man I'd normally consider for a romantic relationship because we are so different. I have a college degree, he has a high school diploma. I like to listen to Kenny Loggins, The Eagles, Adam Levine and Vivaldi, while he likes (the louder the better) Chopin, Italian operas, and Beethoven symphonies. My personality is borderline OCD and hyper-organized, while he's *que sera, sera* relaxed and disorganized. My two sons each live more than a thousand miles away, while he comes from a (redundancy alert) really close Italian family—and has over a dozen relatives who are only about a 30-minute drive from our front door.

I could go on and on, but I've learned that—when it comes to compatibility—those differences don't seem to be what's important. Besides, I've had a number of potentially promising romances that didn't work—despite surface similarities that seemed to signal a perfect fit. So, when I tried to mentally compare him to the other men in my life, I couldn't.

Tony wasn't listed in *Who's Who*, he didn't have a membership to Mensa, and there was no indication that he would ever be a business tycoon. But he did possess a brilliant smile, he owned his own small company, and he had the calmest, kindest temperament I'd ever seen. He loved to cook, play Chopin on his beloved Steinway baby grand, see me smile, and he never—ever!—criticized a single thing about me. Since he firmly believed that all negative behavior is caused by fear, Tony would rarely react with anger or impatience whenever confronted by someone who was acting like a jerk. Instead, he would compassionately—silently—question what that person really feared. And, although divorced (after 30-plus years of marriage), Tony was (and is) free of the unattractive aura of bitterness that clings to so many former spouses.

So, how did this "book client" morph into a sweetheart? Well, the difference between this "friendship first" relationship and my other romances had as much to do with my medically rearranged priorities as it did with the remarkable qualities that make Tony unique.

His elderly mother—like me—was a wheelchair user. (It's politically incorrect these days to say "confined to a wheelchair" even though we both were.) And twice a week or more Tony would unexpectedly drop by her nursing home to share a meal or bring her an opera CD. Soon we were both regular visitors, and watching how he cared for and related to his Mom soon mattered far more to me than his diploma, his IQ score, or the dollar amounts of his investments.

If our unusual love story has an X-factor, it would probably be that, long before Tony and I met, MS had changed almost everything about me, from my appearance to my finances and—particularly—my self-esteem. By the time we met, the personal concerns and goals and priorities that had turbocharged my life for decades had already shifted in a big, big way. The once-active and athletic me (who used to agonize over the perfect pirouette or my show jumping rank at a Saturday horse show), now just remembered and wished. And while "perfect" had once been my favorite adjective, the words I now called upon most often were "courage," "fortitude" and "resiliency." By the time Tony came into my life, I'd begun to long for and fantasize about having (as Dr. Phil calls it) "a soft place to land."

And without even looking—MS and its challenges be damned—I found one. Tony's pleasant phone calls and cheerful visits increased with each passing week. A wheelchair can insidiously create feelings of separation and isolation—especially for a formerly athletic and extroverted woman like me. But he seemed to intuitively know whenever I needed a cabin fever-induced change of scenery or an unexpected activity. Our outings—we were, after all, only "friends"—didn't involve romantic restaurants or expensive getaways. Instead, bookstores, coffee shops and movies were where we'd more and more often spend our evenings and slowly paced Saturdays.

As Tony and I began to spend bigger chunks of time together, it became apparent that my well-disguised anxiety and fear levels were being quietly overshadowed

Of course, getting used to the level of attentiveness and support that Tony brought into my life wasn't easy. I'd had more than a few men say "Goodbye" when I'd been younger, thinner, prettier, healthier—at what I thought was my best. And now, here was someone cherishing me and not wanting to change or improve a single thing, when I couldn't help but feel that—thanks to MS—I was truly at my worst. Oh, Ms. Angelou, you were right—love truly does liberate!

*   *   *

Five years before it aired in Florida, back in January 2008, the BBC One channel began broadcasting one of my all-time favorite British costume dramas, *Lark Rise to Candleford*. It was based on Flora Thompson's trilogy of semi-autobiographical novels that had been published between 1939 and 1943, when England was in the midst of World War II. The BBC series—just like the books—was centered around everyday life in the English countryside during the late 1800s.

Decades after I'd stopped obsessing about the improbability of finding Mr. Right, I was at home in Florida, and sitting next to Tony while we watched TV. I—hopeless Anglophile that I am—was glued to the PBS broadcast of the latest *Lark Rise to Candleford* episode (actually, it was number 21 out of 40). That's when the beautiful, strong, unmarried and wise main character, Dorcas Lane, speaks to her romantically conflicted teenage cousin, Laura Timmons, about love. "I can tell you that to be deceived, to be lied to, and taken for a fool—whatever the reasons—is so painful, so very humiliating that it burns long, long after the heart has healed."

As if I'd been struck by lightning, I was finally able to understand why those long-ago, romantic betrayals had cut so deeply, and had hurt for so long. It had taken me many lonely years to recover from a number of those deep wounds, but I had finally—thankfully—embraced romantic risk for the last time. And, luckily, I'd stumbled upon and found what I'd spent half a lifetime looking for—an emotionally honest, kind man who truly cherished me.

Unlike the younger me, I no longer mourn the departure of those assorted and once-appealing "Ruler of the Universe" Mr. Wrongs because, thanks to them, I was finally able to learn how to both give and accept an honest and healthy form of love. I'd married my first-love high school sweetheart for all the wrong reasons, and had then foolishly given my wounded heart to husband number two because I'd been blinded by his affectionate, glittery, seductive aura. That's why, if anyone had told me—years ago—that I would eventually be a happily married woman who had an equally happily married husband, I would have suggested that they (instead of yours truly) needed to get their brains examined by a top-notch neurologist.

Aware of the ambivalent feelings I had regarding my upcoming milestone birthday, a good friend in

California emailed me this message, which sums up much of what my 65 year old MS-challenged body (and once-weary heart) has learned about love:

> *There comes a point in your life when you realize:*
> > *Who matters,*
> > *Who never did,*
> > *Who won't anymore…*
> > *And who always will.*
> > *So, don't worry about people from your past,*
> > *There's a reason why they didn't make it to*
> > > *your future.*

First Wedding—Vietnam Era

Third Wedding—Clinton Era

Second Wedding—Reagan Era

Sir Gordon Reece

With Sir Tim Rice, 1986

My four perfect grandchildren, 2014

With my family in Palm Beach, 2010

With Tony's family on Thanksgiving, 2011

ENLIGHTENED

CHAPTER 4

I am healthy, beautiful, loved, and **ENLIGHTENED**; happy, famous, rich, and thin.

The aim is first to know, in your head and below it, what you think and feel, and then to reflect on newly unearthed alternatives to your accustomed ways of being.

Jane Howard

Like millions of other Baby Boomers, I grew up in an era when religion was a given for most families in America. But I hadn't even heard the word "Enlightenment" until—in high school—we studied the 18th century movement that emphasized the use of reason to closely evaluate accepted doctrines and traditions. Little did I know then that the adult me would spend more than a few decades reevaluating the philosophical givens of my young years.

Hard as it is to believe today (when Congress' approval rating is hovering around 15%), when I grew up there were certain—practically unquestioned—well-respected struts that supported our middle class world. The Armed Forces, Government, Medicine, and Religion were all considered trustworthy institutions that had our best interest at heart and could be relied upon. Sadly, little by little, that trust has been eroded, and today little (if any) respect is automatically attached to those who are a part of those institutions. These days, bureaucrats, clergy, physicians, as well as high-ranking military officers are frequently viewed either dismissively or skeptically, rather than as individuals who are automatically worthy of our admiration and respect.

But when I was a little girl, which was long before pedophile scandals, punitive malpractice insurance rates, Viet Nam or Watergate, the Clergy played a big role in our family. Daddy had been raised Presbyterian, but Mama was a devout Roman Catholic. And at our house there were three "givens" when it came to God and religion: (1) Attendance at Sunday Mass was non-negotiable, (2) Grace—*Bless us, O Lord, and these Thy gifts, which we are about to receive from Thy bounty, through Christ our Lord. Amen*—was said before each meal, and (3) The religious significance of Easter and Christmas always took precedence over the chocolate bunnies and the gift boxes.

Daddy only accompanied us to church for Midnight Mass on December 24th. The rest of the year he stayed home, and proudly considered himself a Pantheist. In his mind, nature was the ultimate Deity, and no one needed to go inside a church in order to commune with the Divine.

TAOISM: Crap happens.
BUDDHISM: If crap happens, it really isn't crap.
HINDUISM: This crap has happened before.
ISLAM: If crap happens it is the will of Allah.
CATHOLICISM: Crap happens because you deserve it.
PROTESTANTISM: Work harder or crap will happen.
MATERIALIST: He who dies with the most crap wins!
ATHEIST: I can't believe this crap!
JUDAISM: Why does this crap always happen to us?
RASTAFARIANISM: Let's smoke this crap!

* * *

Back when I first began writing celebrity profiles in Los Angeles, I was introduced to a "unique" form of worship thanks to an actor who really felt the need to proselytize about his preferred form of enlightenment. Before I moved to London, my life was literally overflowing with activities and obligations. After a jam-packed workday, I would routinely pull out of the L.A. Times parking lot and race home to (a) drive my sons to the stables where we would each have a one-hour horseback riding lesson, or (b) get to my adult piano lesson on time, or (c) go with my sons to the local Safeway grocery store for our regular marathon food trip, or (d) organize the last-minute details before a dinner party, or—sigh—(e) collapse in a heap on my king-size bed for a few minutes with a good book, and try to recover from the pressure-packed events of the day.

What a hectic schedule like that meant was that there was very little time left over especially for a bookworm like me to watch mainstream TV shows. These days, when the majority of my waking hours are spent in a La-Z-Boy recliner placed strategically close to the television, I have a semi-encyclopedial knowledge about the shows that my cable provider broadcasts. But back then, there were plenty of nights when the TV was never even switched on. And that explains why, when my editor asked me to take Patrick Duffy out to dinner and come back with an exclusive interview, I was pleased—but not overwhelmed.

In fact, before I could even begin familiarizing myself with this latest assignment, a handful of my female colleagues surrounded my desk and begged me to please, please, please bring them an autograph from my session with "Bobby Ewing." It slowly began to dawn on me that Duffy was that season's TV heartthrob on the hit show *Dallas*, and after I calmed down my envious co-workers, I made a beeline to the Morgue to gather clippings and begin my research.

When we met for dinner, Duffy (who was far more attractive and polite than I'd expected him to be) was anxious to tell me about the "magic" that had come into his life ever since he had begun chanting. Back in the late 80s, a number of celebrities (Herbie Hancock, Patrick Swayze, Tina Turner, and several others) were actively involved in Nicheren Buddhism. The popular belief was that by chanting *Nam Myoho Renge Kyo* (Patrick called it "the palace of the ninth consciousness") followers could

*   *   *

Anyone who knows me will be surprised to read what I've written in this chapter, because the people in my life are well aware of the fact that I've always placed religion and sex in the same potentially-awkward soundproof box. In other words, "I would really rather not hear about your feelings or experiences regarding this subject." For years, this has been my own personal "Don't Ask, Don't Tell" policy, and it's been a remarkably effective way for me to minimize unwanted embarrassing or uncomfortable conversations.

As the years went by, figuring out exactly where I stood on the religious issue became an increasingly difficult task. I now realize that what I hungered for was the ability to approach life the way that Dani Shapiro (the inspiring author of *Devotion*) does, i.e., *Recognize the possibility of the Divine in any given moment.*

Years ago, my London editor sent me to Paris to interview the legendary French actress Jeanne Moreau. For years, she had been labeled "The thinking man's sex symbol," and since she would soon be starring in a British TV production, he wanted me to find out what her life in Paris was like. During our three-hour Sunday lunch at a brasserie just across the Seine from the Eiffel Tower, I was blown away by just how intelligent and intuitive she really was. It was like talking to a stylishly dressed, quietly elegant Rhodes Scholar who had lived the most glamorous—but complicated—life, and hadn't forgotten a single thing.

And whenever I find myself grappling with difficult questions (like "How do I get enlightened?"), I think of her cigarette smoke, her shrug, and her throaty voice. And then I remember what she told Oriana Fallaci (another writer who fell under Moreau's spell), "I have always liked things that are difficult. I have always had the urge to open forbidden doors, with a curiosity and an obstinacy that verge on masochism." And could I ever relate to that!

Back in the days when my once well-ordered and enviable life fell apart, and I found myself living alone, hurting, and feeling terrified in London with no safety net and no shoulder to cry on, I had to really scramble to hold it all together. I did not—like Moreau—welcome the difficulties I faced, and I did not—as Mama would have—start offering Novenas or recite the rosary nonstop. Instead, I devoted all of my energy to clinging to what Harvard psychologist Ellen Langer might call "the biology of belief" or "the biology of hope." For me, the only way I could possibly survive was to dump every ounce of energy I had into a basket labeled "Optimism."

Unlike the people who were able to turn to religion as a way of helping them gain everlasting salvation or admittance to Heaven, nearsighted (both literally and figuratively) yours truly sought help in order to better navigate my way through the stormy seas of this life here on earth. There always seemed to be way, way too much on my (present) plate to even think about Eternity. And that sense of overwhelming panic is what brought me to Eckhart Tolle (also born in 1948), the bestselling spiritual author who actually began his career in London. Even though his unorthodox educational background includes Cambridge University and the University of London, Tolle actually conducted most of his studies independently while searching for answers to help him cope with painful and crippling anxiety, depression, and fear.

During my darkest days, I never asked "Why me?" but I did wonder "Why so much?" By any objective measure, in my life up to that point I seemed to have been given way too many "challenges." It was Tolle who helped me reframe what seemed like random catastrophe into extraordinary opportunity. And that's why I still—even now—have this quote from him hanging prominently where I can see it each and every morning: *"Life will give you whatever experience is most helpful for the evolution of your consciousness."*

*   *   *

Eventually, I was lucky enough to find a theological touchstone that satisfied a variety of my (Anglophile, feminist, literary) comfort zones. Julian of Norwich, was a medieval English anchoress who—although she has never been beatified or canonized—is still venerated by the Anglican, Lutheran and Roman Catholic churches. Although very little is known about the details of her life, it is believed that she was born on November 8, 1342, and died around 1416. When Julian of Norwich was 30 years old, she suffered from a severe illness and, as the legend goes, had a series of intense visits from Jesus Christ. She immediately wrote about her visions in a text known as *Revelations of Divine Love*, which included 25 chapters and was about 11,000 words long. It is often referred to as *The Short Text*, and is believed to be the earliest surviving book written in the English language by a woman.

Several decades later, she began to work on a theological explanation of her visions. This book contained 86 chapters, about 63,500 words, and is known as *The Long Text*. Even though she lived in a time of turmoil (The Black Plague, etc.), her theology was based on optimism and a belief in a God whose love was founded on compassion and joy rather than on duty and law. What really drew me to Julian of Norwich was her calming credo, "All shall be well, and all shall be well, and all manner of things shall be well,"

So I chose to make this affirmation the foundation of my (personal) belief system. It is a welcome relief to finally trust that with or without my anxious input, some power—far beyond the grasp of my imagination—is at the helm of our human experience. What a blessing to spiritually exhale and, finally, relax. I no longer worry about attending religious services, chanting, or (like my mother) saying countless rosaries or making novenas. I'm sure Julian of Norwich would have agreed with Meister Eckhart's belief that, "If the only prayer you ever say in your entire life is **Thank You**, it will be **enough**."

*   *   *

With time, I eventually realized that my earlier problems with religion lay in the fact that instead of salvation, what I was really looking for was a usable set of coping skills. I wanted to know how to be wiser, deal with (or better yet, overcome) the emotional, physical and practical issues that challenged me during the day and haunted me at night. And after all these decades, life has finally taught me that we have each been blessed with extraordinary coping skills—it just took me a bit longer than expected to find mine. I offer profound thanks to all the authors of inspiring self-help books and the remarkable survivors—past and present—whose life stories reminded me that Friedrich Nietzsche's most famous quote really is true: *"That which does not kill you makes you stronger."*

Obviously, I am still a long, long way from being truly **ENLIGHTENED**, but I'm close enough to see the glimmer of a spiritual sunrise on the horizon. And I'm so grateful that both fear-of-the-future panic attacks and bygone religious guilt are well on their way to finally being relegated to their future home in my emotional rubbish bin.

As a reluctant retiree, instead of reciting standard prayers I like to "converse" with whatever Universal Force happens to be out there in the Cosmos. And after I've had my say, I like to think that this abbreviated, edited and reorganized version of Max Ehrmann's 1927 prayer *Desiderata* is what She says back to me:

Be yourself.

Remember what peace there may be in silence. As far as possible without surrender be on good   terms with all persons

Keep interested in your career, however humble; it is a real possession in the changing fortunes of time.

Many persons strive for high ideals; and everywhere life is full of heroism.

Take kindly the counsel of the years, gracefully surrendering the things of youth.

Nurture strength of spirit to shield you in sudden misfortune. But do not distress yourself with imaginings.

Therefore be at peace with God, whatever you conceive Him (or Her) to be.

And whether or not it is clear to you, no doubt the universe is unfolding exactly as it should.

In Sister Martha's sixth grade class photo, seated on the far left

Religious Symbols

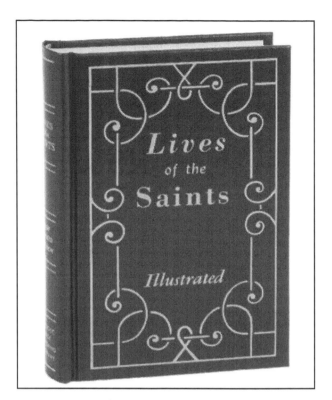

Lives of the Saints

Julian of Norwich

to make peace with being perpetually stuck under the "new girl" microscope, it would have been lovely to have had just a tad more stability—and less change—in my young life.

Obviously, I (and those around me) survived those continual relocations, but I'm willing to bet that there were far more scars than smiles dished out to everyone in my somewhat-crazed, youthful orbit. But before this chapter careens into Jeannette Walls (*The Glass Castle)* territory, let me tell you about the tools I turned to—both as a child and an adult—in my never-ending quest for happiness.

I think it's natural for all parents to want their children to be happy and, fortunately, mine were no exception. In retrospect, I can now see that they gave me what they could, and their best gift of all—a love of reading—has (blessedly) lost none of its luster over the years. At our house, there never seemed to be an excess of money, so I remember clearly—vividly—the few-and-far-between non-book related special gift purchases that were made on my behalf. They included a three-foot doll (blond, of course) with her own wardrobe, a brand-new blue "Murray" (naturally) bicycle, a special embossed leather book bag, a plastic turquoise transistor radio, and a beautiful green silk dress for my thirteenth birthday. Soon afterwards, I was able to earn my own money (by babysitting on weekends, filing in my father's office after summer school classes, etc.) to buy the "extras" that I longed for.

Obviously, the lesson for me was that Mama and Daddy were the type of frugal parents who wanted their daughter to be able to find happiness in places (and activities) that had absolutely nothing to do with the retail experience. Instead, they gave me the most cherished—in our little family, at least—gift of all: a passionate love of the written word. For my first two years with them (until first grade) I was treated to two very special "book sessions" a day. Each afternoon, Mama would tuck me in for an after-lunch nap, and then she'd read me a story. And later, after dinner (while she was doing the dishes, because our homes never had a dishwasher), Daddy would listen as I said my prayers, and then he'd read to me until I drifted off to sleep.

So it's no wonder that as I grew, books became far more than simply bound and numbered pages. Instead, they represented (and evolved into) entertainment, knowledge, love, and safety. They provided answers to my endless questions, and offered ways to help me feel and learn and understand. Whether I was a first grader or a college student or a Senior Citizen, I've always known that as long as I could get my hands on a book—one that would either give me answers or raise new questions— happiness would be within my reach. Reading became my "positive addiction" outlet, and provided me with countless hours of satisfaction. Obviously, Alice Munro knew that same joy when she wrote, "The constant happiness is curiosity."

Back in 1998, Anna Quindlen wrote a short book (*How Reading Changed My Life),* and the entire

In the midst of grabbing all those free, self-help books, I began to understand that **how I chose** to react to the changes and uncertainties of life would essentially determine my level of happiness. It actually felt liberating to accept the idea that (with a little discipline) I could be the author of my own life's story, rather than merely be a supporting character in someone else's. Years later, I truly felt validated when I stumbled across Nora Ephron's edifying quote from her commencement address to the Wellesley class of 1996, "Above all, be the heroine of your life, not the victim."

There's no doubt that millions of other Americans out there are (also) perpetually looking for ways to become happier. And the growing number of *New York Times* bestsellers that have focused on this area (*The Happiest Life, The Happiness Advantage, The Pursuit of Happiness, Stumbling on Happiness,* etc.) proves that there's an endless market of (unsmiling?) consumers who really, really, really want to improve their lives.

Of course, there's no way to write a chapter about being happy without mentioning the bestselling book *The Happiness Project,* written in 2009 by the brilliant author Gretchen Rubin. Rubin's book covers her year-long quest to become happier. During that time, she gave herself month-by-month assignments and then tracked her own progress. Rubin is a first-class overachiever who received both her undergraduate and law degrees from Yale (where she was also editor-in-chief of *The Yale Law Journal*). She then clerked in the U.S. Supreme Court for Justice Sandra Day O'Connor, and she was a chief advisor to

FCC Chairman Reed Hundt. She is a popular blogger, a wife, a mother, and the author of six nonfiction books, but her writing style is so informative, intimate, and open that it's hard to not think of her as a valued fantasy friend. (Can you tell that I have an imaginary long-distance girl crush on Ms. Rubin?)

Before she started work on her happiness book, Rubin encountered a brusque man at a cocktail party who dismissed her quest by saying, "I don't think examining how an ordinary person can become happier is very interesting...I just don't think you're going to have insights that other people would find useful." Now that *The Happiness Project* has been on the bestseller lists for several years and has been translated into eleven languages, I'm pretty sure that she has had the last (happy) laugh!

Rubin wrote, "In the end, I sided with the ancient philosophers and modern scientists who argue that working to be happier is a worthy goal....Contemporary research shows that happy people are more altruistic, more productive, more helpful, more likeable, more creative, more resilient, more interested in others, friendlier, and healthier. Happy people make better friends, colleagues, and citizens. I wanted to be one of those people."

Me, too—no wonder that (forty years earlier) I'd included "Happy" on my wish list!

*   *   *

In addition to my book addiction, a second—particularly quaint—personal "happiness" element would have to be my enduring love of needlepoint. And, like reading, the seeds for this happy-making activity were sown back when I was a little girl.

It all began because Mama had been a great fan of Adlai Stevenson, who—as the bookish and erudite Democratic candidate—had been defeated in both the 1952 and 1956 presidential elections. She'd admired his refined and rather reclusive wife, Ellen Borden, who had gone on record regarding her belief that in order to truly be considered a lady, it was essential for a woman to possess a workable repertoire of needlework skills. Mama may have had little interest in whether or not people considered her "a lady," but she did like the idea of emulating Borden's values. So I grew up surrounded by Mama's chosen sewing skill, which was embroidery. I clearly remember that our dresser scarves and white cotton pillowcases seemed to almost always be decorated with either her tiny, multi-colored flowers or a small, white, satin-stitched "M."

As an adolescent—in order to "overcome" my tomboy tendencies—Mama enrolled me in consecutive crochet, knitting, and sewing classes. Almost immediately, I learned to enjoy the meditative feel of different forms of thread-based creativity. Later, as an adult, I eventually made dozens of knitted sweaters for

118

my sons (as well as for me). And, for years—after lifting my portable sewing machine onto our kitchen table—I would make everything from little-boy flannel pajamas and Halloween costumes, to bathing suits, to Butterick and Vogue-pattern office attire, and (ultimately) even evening gowns.

But the stitching skill that has always seemed to bring me the greatest inner peace and satisfaction is needlepoint—partly because I learned it as an adult (rather than as an awkward adolescent), and partly because it was more of an aesthetic than a practical pastime. One of my most-valued friends, Toni Sherman, patiently taught me how to needlepoint back in the 1970s. At the time, we both had young children of the same age, husbands who travelled a lot, and artistic leanings. So we would spend several evenings together each month, and needlepoint side by side as we caught up with each other's busy lives.

Since that time, I have spent countless hours stitching everything from customized belts to Christmas stockings to chair seats to pillows to rugs to wall hangings. When MS decided to deprive me of the use of my right (stitching and writing) hand, I eventually (and stubbornly) taught myself how to slowly stitch with my left hand instead. Because I'd been raised to "**Always Be Productive and Never Waste Time**," needlepoint has made it possible for me to multi-task to my heart's content. I have stitched while talking on the phone or visiting with friends or watching TV. From finding the ideal canvas to selecting the colors to picking out the yarns to choosing the perfect hand-stitched gift for a friend or family member, every single aspect of creating something beautiful or unique invariably makes me happy. Today, I treasure a small photo album that contains pages full of pictures that capture my completed needlepoint projects, and each finished item has brought me joy both during the process and long afterwards. And (as with reading), it's a *self-defined,* inwardly generated type of happiness—the kind that suits me best!

*   *   *

The third strand of my happiness cable has come—lucky, lucky me—from the friendships I've formed throughout the years. These days—when I am continually connected to and surrounded by a wide variety of caring, entertaining, and thoughtful friends—it really is hard to remember how different things were during my early childhood years. Back in elementary school, I was the solitary little girl who desperately wanted to have friends, but also knew that time (i.e., Daddy's transfers) would inevitably interrupt whatever closeness with a classmate or neighbor might come my way. During those years my most enduring friendships were found on the printed page.

Fortunately, as an adult, I've been blessed to have a near over-abundance of amazing friends. From girls I met in high school to former bosses (even ones from my college days), I am emotionally surrounded by—and deeply grateful for—the kind and generous souls who understand that (more often than not) living with a challenging physical disability can be an isolating experience. I regularly (actually, frequently) hear from cherished friends who are scattered from California to Colorado to Oregon to New York to the U.K., and my nearby Florida friends go out of their way to ensure that I neither am—nor feel—lonely. I know how truly fortunate I am to have scores of people in my life who understand that an unexpected envelope, email, phone call, or visit can transform an otherwise challenging day into one that is easier to bear in every respect. And that shift in perspective—from feeling alone to feeling included— translates into a whole different (and truly welcome) world of happiness. This is not exactly a prayer, but I've always agreed with Marcel Proust's invocation: "Let us be grateful to the people who make us happy; they are the charming gardeners who make our souls blossom."

I am one of those lucky people who can almost always find some event—miniscule or major—that deserves a celebration. It might be a holiday or a friend's birthday, or the arrival of visitors from out of town. Whatever the occasion, there's no doubt that I experience a heightened level of happiness whenever people come to our home for a party. Seeing them seated at our dining table—eating and laughing and talking, perhaps admiring our holiday decorations or the ornaments on our Christmas tree or opening their individual Easter baskets—fills me with an inexplicable (but very real) sense of satisfaction.

And as much as I enjoy the attention and affection of others who come to our home (either individually or in groups), I can always get an extra jolt of happiness just from the knowledge that—at any time—I have the ability to reach out and connect with the people I care about. It's a great source of joy to know that I can still communicate with others (wherever they are and whenever I want) via the internet, snail mail, or the phone.

*   *   *

As both a journalist and an author, I've had the great good fortune to be as happy while involved with the technical (editing, interviewing, researching and writing) side of my work, as when the finished product finally appeared in print. Getting a high five from an (American) editor, a "Well done" from an (English) one, or hearing from readers that they enjoyed an article or book I'd written definitely became addictive.

But after my MS-related health issues sabotaged my journalism career (and the newspaper world went into a tailspin), I couldn't help but miss the positive professional feedback that I'd enjoyed for so many years. Feeling a bit down about no longer having a journalistic outlet (i.e., losing my career-created identity), I stumbled across this quote from Robert Louis Stevenson. *"There is no duty we so much underrate as the duty of being happy."* And no longer seeing my byline in print on a regular basis—the loss of my "platform"—gave me a silly excuse to shirk that duty for far too long.

Luckily, that's when Tony (who by this time was probably getting a bit concerned about his deadline-deprived wife) once again—as he does so often—found a way to make everything better. I had just finished writing my fifth nonfiction book (*The Self-Empowered Woman: 17 Traits of High Achievers*), and was in that limbo land of waiting to see how it would be received. One afternoon, since I'd enjoyed Julie Powell's book *Julie and Julia*, Tony and I decided to go see the eponymous movie as a way to shelve our concerns about what my latest book's future Amazon rankings might be, or what the reviews might say.

We have a specially adapted, wheelchair-accessible van (with a ramp) that allows me to sit next to Tony while he's at the steering wheel. And as we drove back home from the theatre, he turned to me with a big smile on his face. "I can't supply article assignments, intelligent editors, or increased newspaper subscribers for you," he said. "But if you still enjoy or need or want to 'connect' with readers on a regular basis the way you used to, why don't we follow Julie Powell's example and start up a blog?"

As soon as we got home, he created *The Self-Empowered Woman* blog, and my pouting immediately disappeared! And that's how I finally learned the unparalleled joy of generating creative—professional— happiness from within, without depending on ego-soothing feedback from anyone else. By now, I have posted nearly 300 blogs, and written about a wide variety of topics and trailblazers—all of which are designed to inspire other women. After I dictate my (unfortunately) relatively invisible "online column," Tony handles the artwork and the "publishing." These days, there are no executive compliments, expense accounts, hefty paychecks, or high fives. But I can honestly say that selecting the subject, researching the topic, and then writing each one of my short but heartfelt blogs—without fail—places a well-satisfied smile on my face. The simple act of writing my blog—no matter who does or doesn't read it—makes me happy. Obviously, Mahatma Gandhi already knew about that heavenly feeling when he wrote, *"Happiness is when what you think, what you say, and what you do are in harmony."*

* * *

Just as Pharrell Williams' recording of *Happy* was becoming a mega-hit song, I belatedly discovered the Alec Baldwin, Sir Anthony Hopkins, and Jennifer Love Hewitt 2004 movie *Shortcut to Happiness.* Soon afterwards, I dove into Shawn Achors' brilliant book, *Before Happiness.* Obviously, the universe wanted to make sure that I paid close attention to a few important lessons.

Here's a condensed version of the valuable input I received from the convergence of the Happy-centric song, movie, and book:

- Just as Abraham Lincoln noted when he said, "Most folks are about as happy as they make of their mind to be," happiness is a choice.
- Doing things for others (altruism) and being grateful for what you have (gratitude) work like happiness jet-fuel boosters.
- Only 10% of our long-term happiness is based on the external world, but 90% of our long-term happiness is based on how we *perceive* that world.

I've finally learned how counterproductive it was for me to spend so many years hoping that happiness was something I could "get" from other people or from things or even from the outside world. It took nearly a lifetime of learning and living and loving to truly understand that all the tools I really needed to be happy already dwelled deep within me. What a relief to (finally, at 65) learn—as well as understand—that happiness really is a *self-defined* inside job.

I am old enough now to comfortably admit that I have no problem whatsoever with people referring to me as a "Pollyanna." After all, I'm **HAPPY** to confess that I've been called much worse.

One of my ten bookcases

My Wish List in needlepoint

The Self-Empowered Woman

A look at the common characteristics that are shared by high-achieving women from a wide variety of backgrounds with a broad spectrum of accomplishments. It includes self-help exercises and info on 238 women. Purchase "The Self-Empowered Woman" Here

Subscribe To

☐ Posts

☐ Comments

The Self-Empowered Woman
Marilyn Murray Wil...
Best Price $0.01
or Buy New $17.09

 Buy from amazon.com

Privacy Information

Watch Marilyn on YouTube

Followers

Join this site
with Google Friend Connect

Members (78) More »

Already a member? Sign in

Blog Archive

▼ 2014 (13)

  ▼ April (2)

    219: The Self-
    Empowered

SATURDAY, APRIL 12, 2014

219: The Self-Empowered Woman: Idina Menzel

Dear Followers,

First of all, thanks to everyone who has been casting votes on my behalf for the NMEDA contest for a new handicap accessible van. Just in case you need the link (since voting lasts until May 8th), here it is: http://www.mobilityawarenessmonth.com/entrant/marilyn-willison-west-palm-beach-fl/

Now, let me introduce you to one of the entertainment world's most talented **Self-Empowered Women.**

You may have seen her on Broadway in *Rent* or *Wicked*, or you may have watched her on TV's *Glee*, or you may have heard her voice in the animated hit movie *Frozen*, or you may have heard her sing at this year's Academy Awards when John Travolta accidentally mangled her name. The bottom line is that if you've had any contact at all with the entertainment world during the past two decades, you've probably heard **Idina Menzel's** amazing voice.

Born on May 30th, 1971, in Queens, New York, she is the only Tony Award-winning actress to ever record a song (Let It Go) that has reached the top 10. Her grandparents were Russian/Eastern European immigrants, and her mother (Helene) is a therapist and her father (Stuart) worked as a pajama salesman. When she was 15, her parents divorced (**1: No Paternal Safety Net**), and she began working as a wedding and bar mitzvah singer (**2: An Early Sense Of Direction**). Her family is Jewish, and she attended Hebrew school, but didn't have a bat mitzvah (**3: Belief In The Unbelievable**).

She attended NYU's Tisch School of the Arts, and earned an BFA in drama before being cast in the rock musical *Rent*. She was nominated for a Tony Award, but didn't win. Instead, she recorded her first solo

The Self-Empowered Woman Blog
www.MarilynWillison.com

Laughing outake from photo shoot, 2014

FAMOUS

CHAPTER 6

I am healthy, beautiful, loved, and enlightened; happy, **FAMOUS**, rich, and thin

Baby, look at me and tell me what you see, You ain't seen the best of me yet, Give me time, I'll make you forget the rest, (Fame) I'm gonna live forever, Baby, remember my name...

Lyrics from 1980 movie "*Fame*"

I'm embarrassed to admit it, but (as I confessed in the last chapter) there's a small Walter Mitty part of me that has always wanted to be a little bit famous. Not, of course, with the sort of fame that involves a fan club or a complete lack of privacy—just the type that would allow me to feel "special" and enjoy a little bit of public appreciation or acknowledgment for whatever accomplishments I might have achieved.

This life-long ego-driven longing for recognition must have started when my father inundated me with positive reinforcement for anything I did that happened to be—in a good way—out of the ordinary. The first memory I have of receiving this sort of addictive encouragement came when I was in the first grade, and won a contest for reading the most books from our school's small library in a single month. Obviously, they were very easy books (my favorite was the classic children's story *Ferdinand, The Bull*), and—as an inherently competitive six year old—I was delighted to bring home the first-prize reward. Instead of a certificate or a trophy, it was a (much more appealing) ten-inch, multi-colored, giant, all-day lollipop. But the better "prize" for winning that literacy contest was the threefold reward I received from my father. It consisted of the happy look on Daddy's face when I told him that I'd won the competition, his strong warm hug, and the words of praise he directed my way, which made me feel both special and secure.

From then on I was hooked! Any possible opportunity to win approval (or, actually, win anything) became my childhood version of enrollment and full membership in Gamblers Anonymous. Whether it was a Spelling Bee, a Hula Hoop contest, or a short story competition, you could find me (predictably) front and center—hoping to win and terrified of losing. When Richard Costolo (the CEO of Twitter) gave a commencement address at the University of Michigan, he told students: "When you're doing what you love to do, you become resilient because that's the habit you create for yourself. You create a habit of taking chances on yourself and making bold choices in service to doing what

again appears in print—I know that both my ego and my emotional equilibrium will survive. It took me all these years to finally (finally!) learn that chasing after the acceptance and admiration and approval of others—fame—is just a big fat waste of time.

The effort I once expended on trying to get my face and name on display in media outlets has—these days—been diverted. Instead, I now choose to follow the wise advice of the record-setting, marathon swimmer Diana Nyad. On September 2, 2013, at the age of 64, she swam for 53 hours and 110 miles to become the first person ever to swim from Cuba to Key West, Florida. Her musings about fame capture exactly what I've—decades later—learned about the alternative to being famous: "It wasn't so much 'What did I want to do?' [instead] it was 'Who did I want to be?'…Am I living the life that I can *admire*?"

It took a long time (60-some years), and lots of challenging life lessons for me to finally be able to forget about the allure of being "**FAMOUS**," and to work harder at being the type of woman who can answer Nyad's brilliant question with only one word: "Yes!"

Mademoiselle Magazine College Board calendar

Mademmoiselle Magazine College Issue, 1972

First-time cover story and cover girl, 1981

My newspaper masthead archive

Diary Of A Divorced Mother

Diary Of A Divorced Mother--
paperback edition

Time Enough For Love

The Self-Confidence Trick

When Your Life Includes A Wheelchair

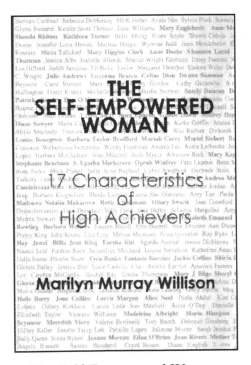

The Self-Empowered Woman

With Sir Paul McCartney in his London office, 1985

With Jackie Collins at London's Ritz Hotel, 1986

where to travel for their next vacation, or which investment strategy to follow.

But over the decades, I've accepted that while certain things (like editing someone else's manuscript or writing my own books) seem to fall into the "easy-peasy effortless" category for me, other tasks—i.e., achieving any sort of lasting financial security—has always seemed to be a Sisyphean challenge. To complicate my troublesome, economic self-esteem, over the years I've enviously watched many of my peers invest wisely, carefully save their money, and then (happily) reap the subsequent economic rewards of a well-thought out fiscal game plan. Their stories, alas, have nothing in common with mine.

Like millions of other women, I loved Sarah Ban Breathnach's 1995 book, *Simple Abundance*, which remained on the *New York Times* bestseller list for more than two years, was translated into 30 languages, and sold millions of copies worldwide. And even though I was already a huge fan of her writing, I was truly unprepared for how much I identified with (and learned from) her beautiful and brutally honest 2010 book *Peace and Plenty: Finding Your Path to Financial Serenity*. That searingly honest volume told readers about her sudden success, newfound astonishing wealth, as well as her painful, personal, and public financial disaster. I've recommended this lyrically insightful book to my girlfriends who aren't affluent, and every single one of them has told me that she found unexpected comfort and solace in its level-headed examination of the disturbing fiscal issues that trouble so many of us.

In Ban Breathnach's words, "*Peace and Plenty* is about women and money. It's an emotionally volatile relationship for most of us. It's also the most complicated relationship we have—and the one that most controls our lives, because we let it. [But] Acknowledging that money is important to you, cherishing and respecting your ability to create and maintain a sustainable flow in your life, handling it wisely so that it can serve you and yours well, and giving thanks for this gift every day during these perilous economic times may seem impossible."

Perhaps the reason that so many financially challenged readers are "able to exhale" after finishing *Peace and Plenty* is because the book introduces us to a wide variety of accomplished, talented women who have come face-to-face with serious money issues. It's an emotional bonus to learn that no matter how badly you may have mismanaged your money or sabotaged your finances, other amazing women before you (like Elizabeth Bowen, Lorraine Bracco, Toni Braxton, Maeve Brennan, Doris Day, Isak Dinesen, Judy Garland, Rumer Godden, Dorothy Parker, Alexandra Penney, Debbie Reynolds, and Rhianna) have all had to cope with their own, harrowing fiscal crises.

*   *   *

In 2013, Lisa Schwarzbaum wrote about women and money in *The New York Times* magazine, "What if I couldn't drum up work, pay my bills, keep the wheels of my life rolling? Who will care about me?...A 2013 survey on women, money and power, issued by the Allianz Life Insurance Company of North America made headlines with its findings that nearly half of all American women fear becoming bag ladies...And the worry is widespread: 56 percent among single women, 54 percent divorced, 47 percent widowed and 43 percent married."

Over the years, I've had enough conversations with those of my peers who are chasing solvency to know that I'm not the only woman on the planet to know what it feels like to have financial fears. Unlike Ban Breathnach's story, my "losses" weren't the result of endless shopping sprees, a lavish lifestyle, or an untrustworthy lover. As for me, every single time I managed (with great effort) to squirrel away a few extra dollars, purchase a bit of income property, or buy a few shares of stock, some urgent event—emergency car problems, unexpected dental work, divorce, home repair bills, unwelcome health nightmares, scary tax issues, or some other lurking economic catastrophe—would ("poof") inevitably swallow up whatever (big or small) amount that I might have managed to set aside.

As Massachusetts Senator Elizabeth Warren and her daughter Amelia Warren Tyagi, wrote in their 2005 book *All Your Worth: The Ultimate Lifetime Money Plan,* "Sometimes things don't go according to plan. Sometimes, even when you are doing your best to put everything together, the pieces just don't work....There are times when bad things happen to good people, times when it seems like you just can't catch a break."

And while I cope with my own level of anxiety about the nonstop and precarious financial burden of hourly-rate, caregiver expenses for my paralyzed body, it's cold comfort to know that I'm definitely not alone when it comes to wrestling with challenging money issues. Mark R. Rank addressed this problem in his book *Chasing the American Dream: Understanding What Shapes Our Futures*. According to his research, almost 40 percent of Americans between the ages of 25 and 60 will experience at least one year below the official poverty line ($23,492 for a family of four), 54 percent will spend a year either in poverty or near poverty, and half of all American children—at some point during their childhood—will live in a family that uses food stamps. Yikes!

As Rank once wrote in *The New York Times*, "Events like losing a job, having work hours cut back, experiencing a family split or developing a serious medical problem all have the potential to throw households into poverty." Fortunately, my financial situation, which is "strained," but neither desperate nor dire—even though I've experienced three of the four challenges listed above—is definitely way below where it should (and where I'd like it to) be.

*   *   *

For me, the bottom line (sorry for the pun) has been that investing, planning, or saving for my future financial well being has simply never—ever—paid off the way I'd hoped it would. This warped economic wariness actually began decades ago, long before I was a Girl Scout Brownie. Prior to even celebrating a double digit birthday, I'd learned how to be suspicious and wary about the rock-solid benefits of "saving for a rainy day."

Back in the late 1950s, Bank of America started a Southern California savings program for elementary school students. Each of us had our own small manila envelope, complete with a string closure on the outside and a pint-sized personalized bankbook on the inside. Every week, we would take our envelopes—with anywhere from a nickel to (far more unusual) "folding money" inside—back to our classroom. Within a matter of days, those envelopes and bankbooks would be returned to us, complete with the new balance that told us (and our parents) what our savings account contained. Just as most of my classmates were doing at their homes, I also pestered Mama and Daddy for additional chores just so that each week I had some sort of change to include in my little Bank of America envelope.

Before I knew it, I'd managed to amass $14, which to my young mind seemed like an impressive bundle of money. So far, so good. But then one of those troublesome, hurry-up "transfers" came along, and our little family had a firm deadline to get to a different state—I can't remember if it was Oregon or Arizona—find a new school for me, locate good dentists and doctors, and select (yet another) house. All went well with our move until I realized that—amidst all the confusion, packing, and upheaval—my hard-won savings account had slipped through the cracks. No one could find either my carefully monitored bankbook or its well-cared for envelope, and in light of all of my parents' far more pressing concerns, that missing $14 barely seemed to matter. But the fact that (over five decades later), I still remember the sting of disappointment regarding the money—**my money**—that had ("poof") just disappeared, suggests that the seeds of my financial distrust and dysfunction probably took root long before I'd learned the definition of either debit or credit.

*   *   *

Today, unfortunately, when I think about money what comes to mind are two things: The first is all the hurtful times when I'd invested, planned, and saved for a specific, future financial outcome only to again (like Charlie Brown, Lucy, and the perpetually yanked-away football) be denied the outcome that I'd optimistically convinced myself would appear. As I mentioned before, it somehow seemed that costly, unexpected—expensive—events would persistently wipe out whatever progress I'd make. And the second "economic emotion" I carry with me is the shame I feel over being (after all these years) unable to figure out a way to keep my physically challenged, financial head above water.

It's become far too easy to torture myself about the money I should have accumulated (but hadn't been able to) over the years when I'd been gainfully employed. Shame on me for always (optimistically and naively) believing that the only thing I ever needed to do in order to have money was simply work—faster, harder, smarter. I never, ever, considered the fact that someday (due to circumstances far beyond my control) I might not be able to either find or do the type of work that gave me so much pleasure and such rewarding paychecks. Like millions of single moms, I'd done my best and worked hard to take care of and support my sons, but I'd been so sure that I would always be able to pay my own way through life that I never even stopped to think about—much less ask myself—"What if?" or "Now what?"

Take it from me, even without being scolded by no-nonsense experts like Suze Orman, it's a real pain to know that you are the least solvent and most challenged (both physically and financially) individual among most of the people in your social circle. As someone who has worked and earned money ever since high school, Orman's words about financially challenged people like me really sting, "It's a simple fact: we tend to spend more when we feel less-than....Fear, shame, and anger are obstacles to wealth....You can turn everything around. You just have to love yourself enough to make it happen." Ouch!

During my last years at the *Los Angeles Times*, I was positive that (once and for all) my painful and problematic money issues had been finally laid to rest. I earned an enviable salary, was part of the newspaper's employee investment plan, had a small but healthy stock portfolio, a beautiful and relatively new car, no credit card debt, and my combined mortgage payment and property tax bill (for a gracious two-story Colonial home) was only $550 per month. When the boys and I moved to London, my sketchy (imaginary) fall-back retirement plan was to "forget about" both my employee investment and stock plans, and let them enjoy an untouched slow but steady growth. I planned to lease my suburban home, buy a new residence in London, work as hard as possible until retirement, save what money I could, and then gracefully enjoy my remaining debt-free "golden years."

Thanks to my charming and generous (but mercurial and demanding) second husband, I had accumulated a pretty impressive collection of "apology"| jewelry gifts, which included amethyst, aquamarine, diamond, emerald, pearl, ruby, and sapphire pieces. In a plan that would make CNBC's (*Mad Money*) Jim Cramer cringe, I had convinced myself that after I turned 65 (in the unimaginable, far off distant future), the imaginary me would be able to comfortably live in my paid-off California home, support myself with the proceeds from my stock portfolio, my fully vested newspaper retirement plan, and Social Security checks. Then—if needed—I could sell one valuable piece of jewelry a year in case I ever needed extra cash for an indulgent treat that might otherwise be above and beyond my annual (fixed) budget.

That pie-in-the-sky plan was foiled by (1) unpredictable (but skyrocketing) interest rates on my London flat's mortgage, (2) thieves who used a sledgehammer to break down our Edwardian front door while the boys were at school and I was at work. They then snatched my "backup retirement fund" jewelry box out of my bedroom dresser, and—"poof"—it was gone, (3) my body's deteriorating mobility and worsening health crisis (which pulverized my once-enviable earning power), and 4) earthquake damage to my California home—which meant that (since I didn't have enough cash to pay for the repairs), my "income property" was no longer safe, and could neither be leased nor rented. In retrospect, I can now see that what I really needed was some good, avuncular advice that could help me "manage" my financial situation. But I was essentially on my own, ricocheting from one economic crisis to the next.

During those scary and lonely days in London, I would often try to bury my panic (no surprise here) by reading as many British periodicals as possible. It was a familiar and affordable form of escapism, and it helped silence the scolding voices in my head. During the Thatcher years, I often saw eye-catching advertisements on the back pages of those glossy magazines that asked readers to (kindly) support a well-meaning charity called "The League for Gentlewomen in Distress." Evidently, it had been designed to come the aid of diplomatic widows or other unfortunate females who had—in spite of their admirable skills, enviable educations, or impressive backgrounds—fallen on hard times. For years—whenever I needed to silence the shame and worry that accompanied my economic insolvency—I'd think of all those unfortunate "strapped but stiff-upper-lipped" female British survivors. The quietly pitied but elegant "Gentlewomen in Distress" were no strangers to the unexpected, unfortunate and unwelcome pain of ("poof") falling on hard times.

Things eventually got so financially perilous that, before I knew it, I'd been forced to cash in my employee retirement fund, sell off my stocks, and (with my tears dropping onto the documents that had been placed in front of me) sign away the deed to the house that I'd always planned on owning forever. Those were the grim days when feeling sorry for myself practically became my full-time job. As Sophie Tucker used to say: "I've been rich, and I've been poor. Rich is better."

*   *   *

As I mentioned before, I've always been woefully unsure of myself when it comes to the whole issue of money, and as I confessed earlier, my problems began long before I knew (or understood) anything about finance. And since Mama and Daddy had survived the Great Depression (The Crash, on October 29, 1929, took place while they were on their honeymoon), my parents always seemed to be comfortable with the frugal lifestyle that colored my childhood.

I didn't inherit an enviable trust fund, astute financial-management skills, or a robust investment portfolio. Instead, Mama and Daddy gave me two skills that haven't made me affluent, but have stayed with me both when I did and when I didn't have money. First of all, they taught me the value of **hard work**. Growing up with parents who were always busy *doing something productive* was a blessing in disguise, because I was expected to (of course) do the same. In our family, being "bored" or "wasting time" was simply not an option. There was always some chore—from cleaning to gardening to organizing to polishing—that was a "better use" of one's time. And the only way to be excused from physically doing something "productive" was to (yes!) read.

The second gift my frequently cash-strapped family gave me was **resourcefulness**. My parents took great pride in being remarkably self-reliant and thrifty. For example, I honestly don't remember anyone ever—ever—being paid to fix or repair or service anything we owned while I was growing up. Chores like fixing the sprinklers or repairing the toaster or refurbishing a screen door would be on Daddy's weekend "Honey-do" list, and Mama's hands—except for her short daily after-lunch nap—seemed to be in constant (if mildly irritated) motion. From baking apple pies to clipping coupons to mending her embroidered linens, she embraced a lifestyle that had far more in common with those from the era of FDR's—rather than JFK's—presidency.

That self-sufficiency mindset was what powered all the "improvement sessions" that were profusely scattered throughout my childhood. From taking Saturday-morning sewing classes, to summertime needlework and knitting lessons, to learning how to change a car's tire, or tie a double-half-hitch knot, Mama and Daddy truly believed that the more practical "life skills" I had, the safer I'd be. And their intentionally edifying, often-repeated messages to me included: "Every problem has a solution," "If you can read you can learn how to do, fix or improve almost anything," and "You don't have to be rich to have a well-lived and worthy life."

*   *   *

In their selfless quest to give me an enviable education, the majority of my hop-scotch school years were spent in private schools among classmates who were usually far more economically advantaged than I. For example, when Sister Cecilia (my pre-teen music instructor who struggled to give me simultaneous violin and piano lessons), happened to be my "then-favorite" teacher, the wealthy father of one of my classmates decided to give all the nuns a memorable Christmas gift. Since he felt that the convent's car—which was owned and used by the nuns who worked so hard to try and educate us—was far too old and way too small for the

Sisters' needs, he gave them—on Christmas Eve, and complete with a giant red bow—a shiny brand-new station wagon. My well-intentioned, standard, two-pound box of assorted chocolates "teacher holiday gift" to Sister Cecilia, of course, paled in comparison. It was one of many (big time) reminders of the deep economic chasm that separated me from my classmates.

Only five years later, at yet another private school in another town in yet another state, I was attending classes with a new group of uniform-wearing teenage girls—some of whom were, once again, way out of my financial league. At that particular school, on the first Friday of each month we were allowed to wear what the nuns called "free dress." To us, it was a rare and enthusiastically welcomed opportunity to feel like we could—one day a month—dress the way that "normal" high school girls did. By then (see: **hard work**), I was old enough to earn money by working for others, and (in retrospect) I can now see that the prospect of finally buying things for myself—things that I really, really wanted to have—made me unstoppably ambitious. As a teenage babysitter (back in the 1960s the standard pay was 50 cents an hour), I had earned a good reputation for being both reliable and responsible, so I was "booked" for most Friday and Saturday nights.

Years earlier, Mama had painstakingly (if somewhat impatiently) taught me what she referred to as "the right way" to iron everything from a pair of my Bermuda shorts to Daddy's starched, white dress shirts. And by the time I was eleven years old, my afternoon routine—even before tackling my homework—was to iron wrinkles out of our family's freshly laundered clothes while standing at the ironing board, and watching Dick Clark's *American Bandstand*. So, as a high school student—in order to earn even more money—I became a mini-entrepreneur by starting an at-home ironing business.

I was well aware that many housewives hated to iron, but for me it was an oddly satisfying chore. After all, (a) I could earn more money than babysitting in the same amount of time, (b) I could make my own schedule and free up those Friday and Saturday nights, (c) I could watch TV, talk on the phone, or even daydream—three things a good babysitter shouldn't do—while still earning money, and (d) as a confirmed clotheshorse, I liked the immediate visual gratification that I got from turning pieces of damp wrinkled fabric into beautifully ironed, ready-to-wear garments.

Ultimately, all those babysitting and ironing jobs paid for a pretty enviable number of different-colored Capezio Jazz Flat shoes, which were that era's version of Tory Burch ballerina flats. For "free dress" day, I might (see: **resourcefulness**) be wearing an outfit that I'd made at home on Mama's Singer sewing machine from a Butterick or Vogue pattern, but my shoes and accessories would easily pass muster with my more privileged classmates. And there were several of those lucky, lucky girls whom—I was sure—couldn't have imagined (in their wildest dreams) ever needing to babysit or iron other people's clothes in order to have extra spending money.

One of my indelible high school memories is of the awe I felt when—for her 16th birthday—my beautiful, blonde, and brilliant classmate, Betsy Marvin, received a brand-new, British-racing-green Porsche from her parents. In contrast, Mama and Daddy's gifts to me for my "Sweet Sixteen" were (1) approval to go on non-group dates with boys, (2) permission to get my driver's license, (3) one of Mama's amazing homemade carrot cakes (my favorite), and (4) an imported lace mantilla to discreetly cover my hair when I went to Sunday Mass.

*　　　　　*　　　　　*

The word "Rich" had first been added to my Seventies-era wish list because—back then—I'd imagined effortlessly having a financially secure, enviable future. It would include big, beautiful homes, brand-new cars, eye-popping jewelry, frequent first-class travel, shopping sprees, a designer-label wardrobe, and plenty of rock-solid investments. It was a foolish fantasy that— Thank God—evaporated into thin air long before I had the chance to become hopelessly smug, spoiled, and superficial.

Even when it comes to my current anemic career as a writer, the tricky subject of money has somehow managed to rear its ugly head. Every month, I receive an appreciated (and much-needed) check as payment for words that I've written, but are secretly published under someone else's name. Believe it or not, in spite of all my financial headaches, for over a decade there have been thousands of readers who evidently pay close attention to my well-researched economic observations. I blush to admit I have been gainfully (but surreptitiously) employed to ghostwrite—each month—a business column about current money-oriented books, developments, and trends. The result is that although I have zero investments of my own, I'm still surprisingly well versed about interest rate trends, the bond market, optimal management techniques, and the long-lasting ramifications of the debt-ceiling crisis. Thanks to my clandestine writing assignments, I'm no stranger to success legends like Napoleon Hill or Tony Hsieh or Christine Lagarde or Sheryl Sandberg, even though I've never even met the manager of the local bank where I have my checking account.

On one of my long-ago interview trips from London to L.A., I had the chance to spend an afternoon (accompanied by my dear high school friend, Karen Bayless) with Angie Dickinson at her beautiful home. Somehow, as the three of us sat in front of her fireplace and enjoyed our chilled white wine, the subject of men, money, and divorce came up. That's when she rolled her eyes heavenward. From 1965 until 1980, Angie had been married to Burt Bacharach, the prolific and successful composer of hits like *"Alfie," "Do You Know the Way to San Jose?"* and *"What the World Needs Now."* But at the time, she was enjoying her own extremely successful career as a TV and movie actress, and the potential residual earning power of her second husband's music was the farthest thing from her mind.

She told me that when she and Burt Bacharach divorced in 1980, she—unfortunately—never even thought about (under California's community property provision) asking for a portion of the royalties from his recording career. But since then—as so often happens—Angie's career (since their divorce) has been far less lucrative than her former husband's. As of 2012, he has had 73 top 40 hits in the U.S., and 52 top 40 hits in the U.K. Can you imagine how she must wince whenever she hears one of his songs in an elevator, a movie, on the radio, or in a TV commercial? I could definitely relate to her wry regret during that California visit, because it had (also) never occurred to me to request alimony from either of my ex-husbands. Like Angie, back then I saw myself as a proud, independent woman who was gainfully employed, and whose future career and earning power were "so bright I had to wear shades." Plus (ha, ha, ha), I was young, ambitious, and extraordinarily healthy.

*   *   *

One result of my financial hurdles (see **resourcefulness**) is that the struggle to remain solvent has turned me into a better-than-average bargain hunter. These days, I no longer have charge accounts at—or credit cards from—Bloomingdale's, Harrod's, Saks 5th Avenue, or Tiffany—the way I used to when money wasn't such a nagging concern. They, too, went "poof." Instead, I've turned bargain hunting for high-end quality goods—i.e., paying a fraction of an item's retail price and doing so in cash—into one of my major pastimes. Who knew, back when I sang *"Second Hand Rose"* in the senior class high school talent show, that I would one day grow up to become a senior-citizen maven at thrift-and consignment-store shopping?

Fortunately, Palm Beach County—where I live—is awash in wealthy residents (and upscale boutiques and merchants) who think nothing of donating beautiful items that happen to be slightly past their fashionable sell-by date to "resale establishments." When I first visited the Sunshine-state (on an assignment from a London magazine editor) I was flabbergasted—in London the phrase would be "gobsmacked"—to discover Burberry and Dolce and Gabbana tops for $30, Ferragamo shoes for $25, Escada blouses for $20, as well as Christian Dior and Oscar de la Renta nightgowns for $15. So, for the past 20 years, I've been (judiciously but happily) buying "expensive" designer bargains while paying Target prices.

My friends feel that I probably use my penny-pinching pastime as a replacement activity for all the challenging (physical) things that my uncooperative body no longer allows me to do, and they may be right. All I know is that I feel an inordinate amount of pleasure whenever I find a "discounted treasure" that I can bring home for only a few dollars. I've found expensive pieces of Italian pottery and Murano glass for $10, Baccarat crystal for under $5, Spode and Portmeirion china for $2, and current bestselling books for $1. On a good day, I can convince myself that it's almost—almost—as much fun as competing in a horse show or completing a series of pirouettes.

What my enjoyment of these bargain-priced treasures means is that—although I am far from being a hoarder—the part of my brain that treasures "things" (the anterior cingulated cortex) is stimulated, in high gear, and very much alive. Obviously, my *"Second Hand Rose"* persona is destined to go on and on!

By turning the art of stretching each and every dollar that comes my way into a game, I've been able to live amidst beautiful things without breaking my budget. And ever-aware that my first priority is being able to pay other people for hours and hours of essential physical care-giving help each and every day, it doesn't bother me to replace retail shopping with the challenges of bargain hunting. A friend of mine, who worked at the Chanel boutique on Worth Avenue in Palm Beach for 25 years, was speechless when I showed her a pair of pristine, black, Chanel ballerina flats from my closet (which—at her shop—would have sold for $800). I'd discovered mine at a local thrift store for $1/100^{th}$ of their retail price—only eight bucks!

On rare occasions, I fantasize about being able to procure—books, clothes, food, household goods, shoes, whatever—without getting stressed about prices. But I've become so accustomed to turning the act of shopping within a strict budget into a competitive game that I'm not sure I could ever go back to blithely ignoring price tags. It just goes to show that when it comes to almost anything in life, less—with time—really can turn into more.

*   *   *

For better or worse, until I was in my 40s, I'd imagined myself to be an outrageously—almost singularly—independent and self-sufficient woman. And until I reached my 60s, I could have never managed to even envision what the life I now live has brought me. Today, my life overflows with extraordinarily generous friends who go out of their way to spontaneously help me cope with the physical and financial challenges that have so drastically altered both my life and my self-image.

What a blessing it is to be surrounded by kind and caring individuals who are sensitive enough to—automatically—ask "What can I do to help?" And then (when I am—as usual—unable to articulate a specific request), they proactively deliver or send or show up to provide exactly what I need. Priceless!

Those unexpected gestures of love (please see the Acknowledgments page), which have come my way from so many of the people in my life, have taught me a number of valuable lessons. And one of those insights has been that the only way I could ever sensibly keep from torturing myself to death (during scary, sleepless nights) about the disparity between how much money it costs to stay afloat when one has a serious chronic illness versus how much money I currently have, would be to stop obsessing and redefine what the word "Rich" really means.

Now that I'm 65, I am truly appreciative and well aware of the fact that while I might not possess much in the way of "usable asset liquidity," I do have a near-overabundance of a much-higher form of powerful currency. My true wealth lies in the kind, loving people in my life who love me without question—even though (unfortunately) I now have very little financial or physical strength left to share with them.

These days, when I inwardly chant my wish-list mantra, I no longer visualize the feelings or even the things that money can buy. As A. A. Gill wrote in *Vanity Fair*, "...the best we can hope for is to be wealthy but to be without cash. Being able to afford everything you desire is not, by any means, the worst thing that can happen to you. But, depressingly, and more profoundly, neither is it the best." Or, as one art dealer told Gill, "If you want to know what God thinks of money, look at the people he gives it to."

In spite of my financial headaches, I've still managed—in my own way—to truly *feel* rich. How? By being able to gratefully acknowledge that although I may not have been able to get what I used to think I really desired (money, money, money), I have been given a different yet wonderful type of wealth.

Life has taught me how to offer profuse thanks (each and every day) for a very special and unexpected gift that actually has nothing to do with being **RICH**. Lucky, lucky me to finally recognize—with apologies to The Rolling Stones—that fate has been kind and generous enough to not give me what I thought I *wanted.* Instead, life has somehow managed to (against all odds) supply me with every single thing that I truly *needed.*

My much-loved California home

Peace and Plenty

With Sir Michael Caine, 1984

My Harrods credit card

First Class work travel

THIN

CHAPTER 8

I am healthy, beautiful, loved, and enlightened; happy, famous, rich, and **THIN.**

You can never be too rich or too thin

Wallis Simpson

Dear Reader, here comes a major Shallow Girl confession: If I had a Fairy Godmother, and we suddenly came face-to-face because she wanted to grant me one magic wish, I'm pretty sure that my choice might surprise you. Believe it or not, I wouldn't ask to get back the use of my muscles so that I could—once and for all—ditch the wheelchair. And I also wouldn't request to have a big bundle of money (miraculously) deposited in my bank account so that my financial worries would be a thing of the past. As you now know, both my fiscal and physical challenges have given me far more than my fair share of pain and discomfort over the years. But, truth be told, their constant annoying static has been like a whisper compared with over 50-years worth of truly superficial,

her most celebrated dessert specialty happened to be light, flaky pies. So, naturally, my always-slim, small-framed father's favorite after-dinner "treat" was a big slice of apple, berry or chocolate pie. During the first years of their long marriage, Mama had worked diligently to learn how to copy her mother-in-law's recipes, so she took great pride in the fact that eventually she managed to flawlessly recreate Daddy's favorite dessert. And if you were to visit my compact Florida kitchen today, you would see—on display—one of the few cherished items I inherited after Mama died: the beautiful, old, worn, wooden rolling pin from the 1800s that had been used by several generations of Murray women to make countless, picture-perfect, flaky pie crusts.

Ok, back to my childhood….Since my mother took such great pride in her decades-long quest to bake beautiful homemade breads and make a variety of flawless pies, the pediatrician's words hit her like a weapon. Mama viewed his innocent suggestion that she curtail my dessert consumption as (unfortunately) an unwelcome prescription that assaulted both her mothering abilities and her hard-won pastry skills. He'd then told her that the only dessert a girl of my "size" needed to eat was fruit. The long-lasting ramifications of his well-meaning pronouncement included a negative ripple effect on (1) the atmosphere at our family's dinner table, (2) our already tenuous mother-daughter relationship, (3) my own feelings about body image, and—ultimately—(4) my appearance-related sense of self-esteem. From that day forward, I was continually reminded (by my disappointed five-foot-one inch mother, who weighed—max—105 pounds) that I was either "big," "heavy," "large," or—more often—merely "unfortunately overweight." For years I had been encouraged to eat far more food than I really wanted to, and now—literally overnight—I was being told that both my appetite and my weight were out of whack.

I usually just let her body-related criticisms dissipate into thin air like dust mites, but every now and then her irritated (and often insensitive) words would cut like a knife. Perhaps the most hurtful comment of all was when (as a high-school sophomore), she—dismissively—told me that I was so big I had "elephant legs." In retrospect, I can now see how ridiculous it was for a very thin mother to tell her fourteen year old daughter (who wore size nine capris) such a hurtful thing. But the truth is, growing up as a "robustly healthy" adolescent with two short and small-boned retirement-age parents had already made me feel physically "different." So it's no surprise that hearing years' worth of incessant negative barbs about both my appearance and my size, torqued my definition of what an "attractive" female body should look like.

*   *   *

Unfortunately, it's now obvious to me that for much of my life I struggled to not see myself as the unlucky, biological hybrid offspring of the overweight and the unattractive. And, naturally, this skewed (and

185

deeply distorted) self-image eventually had a negative impact on many of my relationships, especially the often-doomed romantic ones. For years, I avoided getting involved—no surprise here—with men whom I felt weren't big or strong or tall, because I never (ever) wanted to again be in a situation where someone I was close to might consider me "big." And I know that a small part of the short-sighted reason that I allowed myself to blindly fall in love with my British second husband (who was six foot three), was that his immediate (clairvoyantly seductive) nickname for five foot six inch me was "Tiny Wee."

As I approached adulthood, I gradually realized that my petite mother's critical opinions were (blessedly) not necessarily shared by the rest of the world. I may not have been svelte or skinny, but I wasn't plus-sized either. And (after college) I soon learned that life went on, regardless of what I did (or didn't) weigh. Even though there always seemed to be an extra ten pounds or so that I would fantasize about losing (in order to be more "attractive"), the lure of homemade chocolate chip cookies or a prime rib dinner or guacamole with tortilla chips kept me stuck within the unenviable (but still healthy-looking) body of the medium-sized woman I felt destined (or doomed) to be.

After my first pregnancy, I practically starved myself in order to fit back into my clothes. When I think back on those post-partum days, I remember grimly drinking Carnation Chocolate Instant Breakfast Drink (made with powdered milk and water) every morning for months, and then having lunches that consisted of saltine crackers and a cup of beef bouillon. It was boring and extremely unpleasant, but I had a fast metabolism and enough youthful willpower to make it work. And after my second son was born, I (just like Kim Kardashian did after baby North arrived) used a high-protein low-carb diet to lose the baby weight. When I finally looked like "me again," I gave myself permission to resume my former love affair with regular food.

*   *   *

Now that I have spent close to 25 years in a wheelchair, my (once relatively normal) figure has definitely changed for the worse. Being seated for two and a half decades has (not surprisingly) erased my waistline, and—since MS is the kiss of death to muscle tone—replaced it with a protruding tummy where my flat one used to be. Living with paralysis for so long has belatedly taught me that the body I foolishly berated for so many years (simply because it didn't look "small enough") really wasn't so bad-looking after all. Talk about tortured, 20/20 hindsight!

Back when I was Health and Fitness Editor, my desk would routinely be overflowing with stacks of books about health breakthroughs, exercise and fitness programs, or "new" nutritional-supplement guidelines. Part of my job was to select a weight-loss article or diet book that would then be included as part of each week's packet of copy for our hundreds of international subscribers. So I became (both personally and professionally) familiar with everything from Fasting to Overeaters Anonymous to Weight Watchers, to the Cabbage Soup, Fiber and Grapefruit Diet "slimming" plans.

In spite of being physically active and marginally disciplined about my diet, I was still (not surprisingly) never able to get much smaller than a size ten until I met Judy Mazel, who had just written *The Beverly Hills Diet*. She was 64 years old when she died in 2007, but I will always remember her as a whippet-thin, tiny woman in her mid-30s, who had a huge smile, and an enthusiastically theatrical way of proselytizing about her diet's virtues. When we met, about six months before my second wedding, she blithely promised me that if I would follow her plan and eat (on different days) mountains of pineapple and popcorn and sirloin steak, I could shrink down into a size six for my big day. And she was right!

By the mid-1980s, another book on my messy office desk that really changed my life was *Thin Within* by Judy Wardell, which reduced weight loss to a simple "eat only when desperately hungry" formula. The gist of her program is that we all need to think of our stomach the way we would an automobile's gas gauge, and divide it into ten sections—zero being desperately hungry, and ten being so stuffed that you feel physically ill. According to Judy, anything you eat when you are at level five or above will automatically be converted into fat. So her advice was to wait until you are seriously hungry, eat whatever you want, and then—in order to avoid extra, unwanted "portion distortion" calories—stop eating *before* you reach "hunger gauge" level five.

Several months after I'd syndicated a condensed version of *Thin Within*, I had the chance to meet Judy at the National Convention of the American Book Association in San Francisco. I'd been following her program, had lost ten pounds, and was thrilled to share my success with her. She was—as advertised—slim and sleek and stylishly dressed. Predictably, I became a devoted, lifelong fan when she put her hands on my hips, smiled at me, and then cheerfully said, "But, Marilyn, you don't need to worry about your weight anymore."

Her *Thin Within* plan definitely works, as long as you have the willpower to ignore the tempting sights or smells or thoughts about food during those times when you are not "physically hungry" (above level five). It takes more effort than one might expect to be mindful enough about eating to let your stomach—rather than your brain—control what you put in your mouth. Thanks to Judy, I was again able to comfortably wear size six clothes, but the older I get the harder it is to not be seduced by the prospect of enjoying a treat—whether my stomach's "imaginary gas tank" is below level five or not.

*   *   *

I simply couldn't perpetually eat in such a dictatorial way, but ever since then, as my weight has slowly inched ever upwards, I've used that long-ago "size six" totem as a measurement for how well I'm doing in every other aspect of my life. It's almost as if I've managed to convince myself that the size of my clothes (irrationally) represents either some sort of inner, appetite-control virtue or an external badge of super-human, bodily discipline.

Not that long ago, Kellogg's *Special K* cereal commercials included a scene where women entered a store to buy jeans that were labeled with character traits (like *confident, courageous, fabulous, fierce, radiant, stunning*, etc.) rather than numerical sizes. The theme of the advertising campaign was that we need to remember that we are "More Than a Number," and do I ever wish that message could have been a part of my psyche before I began tormenting myself because I wasn't willowy. But the (inconsequential) fact that I managed to wear size six outfits to both of my sons' high school and college graduation ceremonies remains—especially now that my immobility and "wheelchair weight" issues assault my vanity on a daily basis—a silly (irrational) yet treasured badge of honor.

*   *   *

Professionally, my work as a journalist provided plenty of opportunity to torment myself (over and over and over again) about the fact that I wasn't the size of a starlet. Whether I was interviewing Heather Locklear (*Melrose Place*), Catherine Oxenburg (*Dynasty*), Jane Seymour (*Dr. Quinn Medicine Woman*), or Prima Ballerina Natalia Makarova, there was no way to escape the fact that the entertainment world I was paid to write about seemed to be overpopulated by waif-sized women. After a string of interviews with a variety of performers who wore size-zero outfits that hung on their protruding hip bones, I often wondered what—or if—these women ate.

On one trip from London to L.A., an actress actually—much to my surprise—answered that question. I was scheduled to write a profile of Joan Collins for a magazine cover story, and I learned that she and I would be joined for a luncheon interview by her publicist, Jeffrey Lane. I was amazed to see the slim, super-glam actress enthusiastically order and then consume a large plate of over-easy eggs and French fries. She admitted that she rarely ate such hearty meals because she felt that gaining five pounds made her "look five years older." Afterwards, before our table was cleared, but just as I was putting my tape recorder back into my handbag, she quipped, "I can't believe I ate so much! Tonight I have to wear a black Valentino gown that has a truly miniscule waistline." That's when—as if on cue—Jeffrey turned to her and said, "But, Joan, *you* have a miniscule waistline." And then, just before popping another French fry into her mouth, she smiled, and laughingly answered, "True." I, who hadn't eaten a French fry in close to 15 years, left the interview with plenty of good quotes for my editor, and proof that some actresses do (occasionally) consume calories.

*   *   *

One of the side effects of America's obesity epidemic is a whole new genre of size-centric TV programs. Shows like *My Big Fat Revenge, Dance Your Ass Off, Extreme Weight Loss,* and *The Biggest Loser* have introduced viewers to seriously overweight people who are willing to endure practically anything in order to (finally) be smaller. I've never been large enough to even think about qualifying as a contestant for any of those shows, but (still) I sit glued in front of the TV, mesmerized by their anguish, and happy to watch them enthusiastically worship at the altar of Slim.

People on those programs—who really do seem to suffer—like to say that all they really care about is getting healthy. But it's hard for me to not wonder if their motivation goes way beyond improved health markers, and delves into deeper emotional levels. Recently, comedian Sarah Silverman told columnist Maureen Dowd that in America, comedy and gender and size are all related: "Look, Jonah Hill can be fat, guys can be fat and still deserve love in this society…In white America, overweight women don't deserve love."

And if today's images of super-skinny females in magazines and on fashion-show runways aren't irritating

192

enough, TV shows in general have now become the new weapon of torture for women like me who are irrationally obsessed with body size. There is a cabal of skinny media-queen celebrities (on both network and cable TV stations) who seem to somehow have it all. They're affluent, they're attractive, they're mothers, the public seems to love them, they're successful in their fields, and—ouch—they're really skinny. Not a single friend of mine is particularly interested in or fascinated by these tiny tycoons, but I continue to be (hopelessly) obsessed by all those women in media who seem to have super-human willpower when it comes to food.

Unfortunately, these days the majority of my time is spent in a La-Z-Boy recliner where—at any given moment—I can turn on my TV and ogle the fat-free physiques of (exercise guru) Tracy Anderson, (designer and former Spice Girl) Victoria Beckham, (Skinnygirl mogul and former talk show host) Bethenny Frankel, (Goop blogger and Academy Award winning actress) Gwyneth Paltrow, and (stylist and reality show star) Rachel Zoe—not to mention Guiliana Rancic, Kelly Ripa, or Tori Spelling. I'll always remember how whippet thin Rose Byrne and Emma Stone looked when they appeared on Jimmy Fallon's *The Tonight Show*. And who can forget those super-skinny *Desperate Housewives*?

A few years ago, I met Camille Grammer (formerly of *The Real Housewives of Beverly Hills*) and Lisa Vanderpump (of *Vanderpump Rules*), and was shocked by how tiny they seemed in person. (Silly me to have forgotten that the camera automatically adds an extra ten pounds—so if someone looks thin on TV, in person she will be much, much smaller.) As we sat next to each other, I couldn't help but notice that my wrist seemed twice as large as Camille's and, compared to Lisa, it was hard for me to not feel like an overweight Amazon trapped in a black vinyl wheelchair.

*   *   *

Currently, there are over 20,000 diet and weight loss books listed on Amazon, and my friends tease me whenever I insist on learning about the latest "way" to lose weight. In spite of having read hundreds of diet books, I still am not (surprise, surprise, surprise) as trim as I'd like to be. My long-standing "size obsession" has, alas, morphed into genuine and obvious self-consciousness about my heft. Lusting after a size six figure will probably always be a part of my twisted, image-conscious psyche. But even though my desire may be strong, my aging MS-challenged body (in more ways than one) is weak.

Since I'm no longer able to stand on a scale (and probably wouldn't want to), I don't even know what I weigh these days, but I am acutely aware that in order for my body to get from one place to another it must be lifted by another person. This chore (sadly) falls to someone who is strong, hopefully kind, and—of course—being compensated by an hourly wage. Thanks to this awkward and repetitive procedure, I am aware of the fact that I am no featherweight. Every trip (to the bathroom, to physical therapy, to leave the confines of my home, or to escape from either my recliner or my wheelchair) means that my uncooperative body must be lifted (i.e. transferred) and then repositioned. And while it's not exactly an appetite suppressant, it does serve as a self-conscious reminder that what I weigh these days directly affects other people's lives as much as my own.

Perhaps that's why—when it comes to the struggle to control my weight—I keep the late Senator Ted Kennedy's words (which were directed towards a far more worthy goal than shrinking one's physical size) on display: "The work goes on, the cause endures, the hope still lives, and the dream shall never die."

*   *   *

For the past year or so, I've been a disciple of the English medical journalist Dr. Michael Mosley's study on intermittent fasting. His program, which was broadcast on PBS and is outlined in the internationally bestselling book *The Fast Diet*, suggests that giving our body an "intermittent fast" from food reduces the risk of everything from cancer to cardiovascular disease to diabetes. His plan requires two food-restricted (500-600 calories) days each week, which are designed to help give the body a chance to reset its metabolism.

Since Tony and I never know which days of the week will involve unexpected schedule changes or visitors, we prefer David Zinczenko's *The 8-Hour Diet* plan because all we have to do is limit our chosen food intake to an eight-hour span each day. This gives us sixteen calorie-free hours so that our bodies can (theoretically) cleanse, repair, rest, and reset our metabolic rate. There's quite a bit of research that indicates "intermittent fasting" can also help fight Alzheimer's and improve human growth hormone levels. Eating that way for the past 18 months has not given me the rail-thin body I'd like to have. Still, I haven't gained, I may even have lost (if the way my clothes fit can be considered "feedback") a few pounds, and (super-slim) Tony and I are both happy with its invisible internal effects.

Naturally, having an enviable body when you also have MS is a real challenge. And while I do get plenty of regular physical therapy, the fact remains that (for me) adequate exercise is practically impossible when (a) you only have the (limited) use of one arm, (b) movement (i.e., working out) is essentially impossible, and (c) what little remaining muscle tissue you do still have is slowly (day by day) atrophying. So, even if I were to get each and every one of my emotional appetite issues under control, what I'd be left with would probably be a different—equally disturbing—problem.

On Chris Powell's *Extreme Makeover* TV program, contestants work for one full year to lose close to half their weight. But they then need to have major surgery in order to remove the "excess loose skin" that remains. And—yikes!—even if I were lucky enough to squeeze into a size six once again, I'd probably be faced with a junior version of the "skin problem" that Chris Powell's success stories need to deal with after their transformation. And both my fear of scalpels and tight budget means that skin reduction plastic surgery is nowhere to be seen on my future horizon.

*　　　　*　　　　*

Starting back in the 1980s, size and weight seemed to become as much of a status issue as a health concern. Author Tom Wolfe (in his brilliant fictional depiction of Manhattan multi-millionaires, *Bonfire of The Vanities*) poked fun at the wealthy women who met for lunch, but never ate. He called them "Social X-rays," and from that moment on it seemed as if our culture adopted a knee-jerk, judgmental conclusion that automatically equated *willowy* with *willpower* and *large* with *lack of discipline*.

While I still harbor occasional fantasies about looking like a human clothes hanger, my birthday wish to myself this year is to finally accept—and embrace—the body I have today. I'm pretty sure that I have (thanks to MS) far bigger body concerns (and problems) ahead of me than the fact that I can no longer fit into a single-digit wardrobe. But here is where—at 65—I will confess that the fantasy of having frail-looking "cigarette arms," long slim legs, and the enviable waistline that I used to have will probably never lose its allure or appeal.

While making the film *Dallas Buyers Club*, actor Matthew McConaughey lost 47 pounds, and—in order to portray the transsexual character, Rayon—Jared Leto dieted away about 30. By the time Leto appeared on the movie set, the five foot nine inch actor weighed only 116 pounds. Even though the last time I saw such a small number on the scales was during my freshman year in high school, I totally understood his feelings about achieving such a drastic weight loss. He admitted that being skinny "…changes the way you walk and talk and think and feel, the way people treat you, [and] the choices you make."

Ages ago, thanks again to *PBS*, I learned about Dr. Joel Fuhrman and his micronutrient-rich *Eat To Live* plan. For years, he has advocated using a simple formula known as H=N/C, which stands for "Health=Nutrition divided by Calories." Fuhrman calls this program nutritarianism, and it is the basis of his latest book (his eighth), *The End of Dieting*. The idea is—for those of us who want to lose weight and get healthier—to flood the body with so many micronutrients that we no longer crave empty or toxic calories. I really like the idea that being able to eat unrestricted amounts of "good for you" foods might actually be—finally!—the end of dieting.

But then, just when I thought I knew everything there was to know about nutrition and weight loss, along came *The Bulletproof* Diet by Dave Asprey. That's when my lifelong quest for a smaller size and a lower number on the scale took a radical "fat versus sugar" turn. These days, I begin each morning with a strong cup of Bulletproof coffee, but that elusive size six still seems far, far away…

Fortunately, I have just enough mental and physical strength left to finally appreciate and be grateful for (on a daily basis) who I am, what I still can do, how I look, and the life I have. And that's the rock-solid truth, no matter what size clothes I might happen to wear or how **THIN** I may (or may not) be—now that I'm 65.

Chubby me, 1953

The Beverly Hills Diet

Thin Within

With Jane Seymour at St. Catherine's Court, 1986

Size six graduation photos with my sons

With Lisa Vanderpump in Beverly Hills, 2013

The End of Dieting

EPILOGUE

The business of life is the acquisition of memories. In the end, that's all there is.

Mister Carson *Downton Abbey*

The same week that I finally completed writing down a year-long reevaluation of my almost-septuagenarian life story, my fellow book-loving friend, Donna Brown Agins, called from San Diego with an enthusiastic suggestion. She wanted me to get my hands on Jane Pauley's second nonfiction book *Your Life Calling: Reimagining the Rest of Your Life*. Donna felt that Pauley's volume—and the one I had just finished writing—addressed several of the same issues, particularly Baby Boomer change and reinvention. As usual, Donna was right.

And while deep into the pages of Ms. Pauley's book, I was lucky enough to come across this quote from novelist Elizabeth Crook. "Looking back on [your] life is like seeing a movie for the second time. You notice things that you didn't see the first time; you can see how this led

204

up to that part of the story…when we look back, we can see things that were there all along." Her words described exactly what I had experienced during the process of putting together this memoir.

My roller-coaster life—like those of so many people I know—has had very little in common with what my younger self thought "the future" would be like. And while I used to think that getting older was primarily the gradual accumulation of assets, birthdays and experiences, I now know two important things about aging. First, the passing years tend to present us with challenges. Then, time allows us to incorporate, as well as manifest, highly individualized coping skills—like adaptation, survival and (if we're lucky) wisdom.

In my case, the duality of age and illness has delivered an unexpected surplus of blessings, burdens, and gifts right to my doorstep. Thanks to MS, I'm well aware that there is no way to even begin to reclaim the action-packed life that I used to have (or the hyper-productive me I used to be). But there is also no way to deny the welcome feeling I get each day—in spite of my paralysis—that there is still a world full of wonderful things left for me to do.

I've learned (finally) that this is the stage of life when it's really important for me to focus—rather than squander—whatever available energy and time that I still have at my disposal. As "seasoned women" we can all compress our age-altered abilities to both improve our own situation and positively affect the lives of others.

And this Senior Citizen awareness brings with it a treasured sense of excited—anticipatory—urgency that adds a welcome texture to the flavor of each and every day. It's almost as if turning 65 has been as unexpectedly exciting as cracking open the tight covers of a longed-for brand new book.

This is the welcome stage of life when it makes sense for all of us to remember the challenge that H Jackson Brown, Jr. gave his college-bound son in the pages of *Life's Little Instruction Book*. "Don't say you don't have enough time. You have exactly the same number of hours per day that were given to Helen Keller, Louis Pasteur, Michelangelo, Mother Theresa, Leonardo da Vinci, Thomas Jefferson and Albert Einstein." No matter how old (or young) we happen to be, this is the time to work at making every hour and each day worthwhile.

If nothing else, the (many) decades I've lived have finally taught me the value of consciously choosing to meet everything with an open heart, which has often been referred to—or defined—as "acceptance." After all, the truly wise seniors among us seem to already know that all great life lessons come our way for a specific purpose. Even though they tend to be—more often than not—camouflaged as obstacles, they invariably arrive as uninvited vehicles specifically designed to give us custom-made much-needed opportunities for growth.

Recently, while smack in the middle of reading Ann Patchett's beautiful book *This Is the Story of a Happy Marriage*, I stumbled across this excerpt from her 2005 convocation address to The Miami University of Ohio, "We all turn our lives into stories. It's the defining characteristic of our species....Just as every story we tell bears our own distinctive slant on the experience, every story we read bears someone else's....The writer has made a decision on what to include and what to leave out. It doesn't mean he or she isn't telling the truth; it simply means that events can't be recorded exactly. They can only be interpreted. Even a photograph reveals only part of the picture....Whom do you choose to leave out of the portrait? Whom do you choose to include?"

No doubt there are people in my life who will ask those questions about the book you're holding, which is my first foray into "memoir world." And since this has been a tentative attempt to analyze and tell my own life story, it is sure to have more than its fair share of flaws. But the once-troubling prospect of turning 65 presented me with the perfect opportunity to revisit the people, places and things that help shaped my life. And—at this point in time—that process now seems almost like a retrospective bonus gift for having survived everything that fate happened to throw my way. What a relief it has been to finally understand that (especially for people who are dreamers) growing older and moving forward in life rarely follows a predictable or uncomplicated path.

I am, of course, profoundly grateful to have had the privilege of—so far—experiencing an extremely full and multi-layered life. And, instead of feeling "older," "elderly," or even like an authentic "Senior Citizen" simply because I'm 65, I now sense the arrival of an unexpected—and very welcome—new beginning. After all, I've already navigated my way through so many major-league life challenges that whatever I choose to tackle next can only be a delicious new chapter. No wonder I have always agreed with C.S. Lewis' wise observation that "You are never too old to set another goal or dream another dream."

Like millions of other readers over the past 25 years, I've long been a vocal fan of Paulo Coelho's *The Alchemist*. This small volume—which when first published sold only a handful of books—has now been translated into almost 60 languages, has been on *The New York Times'* bestseller list for over 300 consecutive weeks, and has sold over 65 million copies. Obviously, we all want to believe that, "…there is one great truth on this planet: whoever you are, or whatever it is that you do, when you really want something, it's because that desire originated in the soul of the universe. It's your mission on earth…when you want something, all the universe conspires in helping you to achieve it."

What a surprise to discover that instead of being a mere fantasy, my wish list (*healthy, beautiful, loved, and enlightened; happy, famous, rich, and thin*) was not simply the product of my collegiate imagination. It had evolved—over the course of forty years—into far more than an emotional Rescue Remedy mantra. Instead, it grew from simply being a series of aspirational words into the customized story that I chose to tell my present self about my future self.

What's your customized story?

ACKNOWLEDGMENTS

It's no secret that ever since MS hijacked my body's mobility, my days seem to revolve around and depend upon the kindness of others. Their concern and support are essential components of the collaborative and creative process that defines the altered way I now live my life. It almost feels as if—in order to do justice to all the helpful hands-on people who were involved with these pages—I would need to create an equally lengthy "tribute volume" to acknowledge their contributions. Since that is (obviously) not practical, I can only hope that the following list will serve as a well-meant replacement...

Deepest thanks to:

Toni Sherman and **Tom Safran,** for their astonishing affection, generosity and support.

Donna Brown Agins, who—literally—made this book possible.

Howard Schiff, John Servideo and Sandra Gadow for essential (and good-natured) editing, and typing (and re-typing) assistance.

Sonia Cooper, Chief Instigator and Marketing Maven, and the tireless **Elizabeth Varian** for their superior website creativity and social media support.

The amazing **Laura Lynch,** for her reliable Facebook maintenance, internet skills and remarkable layout talent. Laura, you never fail to astonish me.

My long-distance cheerleading squad, which includes **Helen Bass, Karen Bayless, Hilary Gauntt, Mary Jobes, Terry Orth, Anne Rodgers** and **Susan Schorr.**

My Florida first-readers and support squad— **Bobby Dougherty, Sue Fleming, Jeanne Hogue, Kelli Jacobs, Bea Lewis, Donna Marks, Lisa Murphy, Ellen O'Bannon, Parama, Rita Romano** and **Catherine Van Ormer.**

All the **Fragiacomo** and **Willison** family members who lovingly worked overtime to help keep me connected and on track.

Lastly, to my astonishingly dedicated, devoted, and patient husband, **Tony**, who continues to provide more essential intangibles than I could have imagined would ever come my way.

LIST OF BOOKS BY CHAPTER

INTRODUCTION

The Secret by Rhonda Byrne (Atria Books/Beyond Words, 2006)
Think and Grow Rich by Napoleon Hill (Tarcher, 2005)
The Power of Positive Thinking by Norman Vincent Peale (Touchstone , 2003)
Glitter and Glue by Kelly Corrigan (Ballantine Books, 2014)

HEALTHY

Le Rouge et le Noir by Stendahl (*The Red and The Black*, Penguin, 2003)
The French Lieutenant's Woman by John Fowles (Back Bay Books, 1998)
Let's Get Well by Adele Davis (Signet, 1988)
Passages by Gail Sheehy (Ballantine Books, 2006)
Counterclockwise by Lauren Kessler (Rodale Books, 2013)
Jane Eyre by Charlotte Bronte (CreateSpace Publishing, 2014)

Learned Optimism by Martin Seligman (Vintage, 2006)
Crazy Sexy Cancer by Kris Carr (Skirt, 2007)
Obsessed by Mika Brzezinski (Weinstein Books, 2013)

BEAUTIFUL

Gone with the Wind by Margaret Mitchell (Warner Books, 2000)
I'm Dancing As Fast As I Can by Barbara Gordon (Moyer Bell, 2011)
Cinderella Ate My Daughter by Peggy Orenstein (Harper Paperbacks, 2012)
Madame by Patrick O'Higgins (Viking Press, 1971)

LOVED

The 5 Love Languages by Dr. Gary Chapman (Northfield Publishing, 2009)
Cured: My Ovarian Cancer Story by Joyce Wadler (e-Quality Press, 2013)
Eat, Pray, Love by Elizabeth Gilbert (Penguin Books, 2007)
Committed: A Skeptic Makes Peace with Marriage by Elizabeth Gilbert
(Penguin Books, 2011)
Lark Rise to Candelford by Fiora Thompsom
(David R. Godine; First Godine Edition, March 1, 2010)

A Homemade Life by Molly Wizenberg (Simon & Schuster, 2009)

ENLIGHTENED

Lives of the Saints (Catholic Book Publishing Corp, 1993)
Devotion by Dani Shapiro (Harper Perennial Reprint, 2011)
The Short Text by Julian of Norwich (Penguin Books, 1999)
Revelations of Divine Love by Julian of Norwich (Penguin Books, 1999)
The Long Text by Julian of Norwich (Penguin Books, 1999)
Desiderata by Max Ehrmann (Crown, 1995)

HAPPY

Nicholas Nickleby by Charles Dickens (Wordsworth Editions, 1998)
And Never Stop Dancing by Gordon Livingston (DeCapo Lifelong Books, 2008)
The Glass Castle by Jeannette Walls (Scribner, Reprint Edition, 2006)
How Reading Changed My Life by Anna Quindlen (Ballantine Books, 1998)
My Life in Middlemarch by Rebecca Mead (Crown, 2014)
The Happiest Life by Hugh Hewitt (Thomas Nelson, 2013)

The Happiness Advantage by Shawn Achor (Crown Business, 2010)

The Pursuit of Happiness by Chris Gardner and Quincy Troupe (Amistad, 2006)

Stumbling on Happiness by Daniel Gilbert (Vintage, 2007)

The Happiness Project by Gretchen Rubin (Harper Paperbacks, 2011)

The Self-Empowered Woman: 17 Traits of High Achievers by Marilyn Murray Willison (BookSurge Publisher, 2009)

Julie and Julia by Julie Powell (Back Bay Books, 2006)

Before Happiness by Shawn Achor (Virgin Books, 2013)

FAMOUS

Ferdinand, The Bull by Munro Leaf and Robert Lawson (Grosset & Dunlop, 2011)

Diary of a Divorced Mother by Marilyn Murray Willison (Wyden Books, 1980)

The Chronicles of Narnia by C.S. Lewis (Harper Collins, 2010)

This Is the Story of a Happy Marriage by Ann Patchett (Harper, 2013)

The Self-Confidence Trick by Marilyn Murray Willison (Weidenfeld Nicolson, 1988)

The Importance of Being Famous by Maureen Orth (Henry Holt & Co., 2004)

RICH

Little Men by Louisa May Alcott (Puffin, 1995)

Simple Abundance by Sarah Ban Breathnach
(Grand Central Publishing, 2009)
**Peace and Plenty: Finding Your Path to
Financial Serenity** by Sarah Ban Breathnach
(Grand Central Publishing, 2010)
**All Your Wealth: The Ultimate Lifetime Money
Plan** by Elizabeth Warren and Amelia Warren
Tyagi (Free Press, 2006)
**Chasing the American Dream: Understanding
What Shapes Our Futures** by Mark R. Rank
(Oxford University Press, 2014)

THIN

The New Beverly Hills Diet by Judy Mazel (HCI
revised edition, 1996)
Thin Within by Judy Wardell (Random House,
1997)
The Fast Diet by Michael Mosley (Altria Books,
2013)
The 8-Hour Diet by David Zinczenko (Rodale
Books, 2012)
Bonfire of the Vanities by Tom Wolfe (Picador,
Reprint Edition, 2008)
Eat To Live by Joel Fuhrman, MD (Little Brown
and Company, 2003)
The End of Dieting by Joel Fuhrman, M.D.
(HarperOne, 2014)
The Bulletproof Diet by Dave Asprey (Rodale,
2014)

EPILOGUE

    Your Life Calling by Jane Pauley (Simon & Schuster, 2014)

Life's Little Instruction Book by H. Jackson Brown, Jr. (HarperCollins, 1991)

This Is the Story of a Happy Marriage by Ann Patchett (Harper, 2013)

The Alchemist by Paulo Coelho (HarperCollins, 1993)